Current Perspectives:
Readings from InfoTrac® College Edition

Racial Profiling

RODNEY BRUNSON
University of Alabama at Birmingham

THOMSON
™
WADSWORTH

Australia • Brazil • Canada • Mexico • Singapore • Spain
United Kingdom • United States

THOMSON
™
WADSWORTH

Current Perspectives: Readings from InfoTrac® College Edition
Racial Profiling
Rodney Brunson

Executive Editor: *Marcus Boggs*
Acquisitions Editor: *Carolyn Henderson-Meier*
Assistant Editor: *Meaghan Banks*
Marketing Manager: *Terra Schultz*
Marketing Communications Manager: *Tami Strang*
Project Manager, Editorial Production: *Samen Iqbal*
Creative Director: *Rob Hugel*
Art Director: *Maria Epes*

Print Buyer: *Becky Cross*
Permissions Editor: *Mardell Glinski Schultz*
Production Service: *Ruchika Vij, ICC Macmillan Inc.*
Copy Editor: *Heather Mann*
Cover Designer: *Larry Didona*
Cover Image: *Photolibrary.com/Photonica*
Compositor: *ICC Macmillan Inc.*

Printed in the United States of America

1 2 3 4 5 6 7 11 10 09 08 07

Library of Congress Control Number:
2007934466

Student Edition:
ISBN-13: 978-0-495-10383-7
ISBN-10: 0-495-10383-7

For more information about our products, contact us at:
Thomson Learning Academic Resource Center
1-800-423-0563

For permission to use material from this text or product, submit a request online at
http://www.thomsonrights.com.
Any additional questions about permissions can be submitted by e-mail to
thomsonrights@thomson.com.
Thomson Higher Education
10 Davis Drive
Belmont, CA 94002-3098 USA

Contents

Search and Seizure   111

Preface

RACIALLY BIASED POLICING

For several decades disadvantaged Black citizens have frequently reported being unjustly stopped and searched by the police. However, it was not until similar complaints were registered by a number of high profile African Americans that law enforcement executives began to take the issue seriously. Scholars and policymakers also have recently begun to examine the nature and extent of racial profiling in several jurisdictions across the United States. In addition, the federal government, along with a growing number of state and local law enforcement agencies, has vehemently denounced the practice. While such declarations and associated policy changes are politically correct and appeasing to some, they cannot ensure that minority citizens will be protected from discriminatory policing practices.

Although racial profiling research has become increasingly popular, the vast majority of studies have relied upon survey or official data to document the frequency of stops experienced by members of various racial groups. Thus, many researchers have faced difficulty in determining whether citizens are being stopped in proportion to a particular baseline measure (e.g., the number of licensed drivers, registered voters, vehicle owners). While these studies have highlighted important race differences, examining the racial composition of individuals stopped by the police alone will yield few long-term benefits. In particular, traffic stop statistics may tell only part of the story because such data fails to fully capture the complexity of minority citizen/police relations and prevents us from obtaining an understanding of what takes place during these encounters.

This reader has been assembled to supplement multiple Wadsworth texts, and features articles available via Wadsworth InfoTrac® College Edition. In addition, the collection of articles is intended to highlight the current perspectives on racially biased policing. These pieces have been chosen in hope of highlighting a wide range of discriminatory policing practices and their consequences. Therefore, the reader is divided in four parts: racially biased policing, contemporary racial profiling, Hispanic immigration, and search and seizure.

The first set of articles examines Black citizens' disproportionate experiences with aggressive policing initiatives. For example, "Policing Space, Policing

Race: Social Control Imperatives and Police Discretionary Decisions," highlights the tenuous relationship that exists between African Americans and the police. In addition, the article details how official and unofficial police patrols historically have been used to enforce discriminatory laws and limit Black citizens' movement. And "Race and Policing," suggests that aggressive policing strategies have resulted in substantial crime reductions in certain locales. The piece cautions, however, that the harmful byproducts of race-based policing erodes trust and ultimately undermines effective crime control efforts. Black citizens' widespread negative feelings about the legitimacy of police stops have perhaps contributed to the phenomenon aptly referred to as DWB (driving while black). Studies have found that Blacks were more likely than Hispanics or whites to believe they were unjustly targeted by police and mistreated during such encounters.

The next handful of articles illustrates how the threat of terrorism following September 11 has changed the tenor of public discussions about racial profiling. For example, "Flying While Arab: Lessons from the Racial Profiling Controversy," notes how racial profiling efforts in the U.S. have been extended beyond Blacks and Hispanics and currently focuses on Arabs, Muslims, and those of Middle Eastern descent. In particular, the article reminds us that past racial profiling initiatives failed and in the process violated many immigrants' civil liberties. Also, "Last Week, Profiling Was Wrong," examines whether heightened national security concerns have made racially biased policing more palatable to scores of Americans.

The third series of articles demonstrate that there is considerable interest in the U.S. regarding the pace of immigration and immigration policy. In particular, these articles examine assimilation processes among a rapidly growing Hispanic immigrant population. However, in the aftermath of September 11, discussions of immigration have now turned toward determining the moral fitness of those seeking to legally enter the country. Thus, there is considerable interest in the extent and nature of foreign-born persons' involvement in crime. Whereas immigrants' arrest and incarceration rates have important implications for crime control efforts, so do their relationships with law enforcement personnel. A growing body of research has begun to examine immigrant/police relations. In addition, scholars have considered whether or not group members' feelings about justice processes in their native countries influence their perceptions of U.S. police authorities.

The final set of articles investigates how police powers are used during vehicle stops. These pieces especially highlight the implications that recent U.S. Supreme Court rulings have for police search and seizure procedures. In particular, "State of the Stop," explores a wide range of issues involving police searches incident to arrest and questions whether a series of related Supreme Court rulings have methodically whittled away Fourth Amendment protections.

Citizen trust of the police is an important issue because allegations of misconduct have the potential to undermine the legitimacy of law enforcement officers and to reduce public confidence in the criminal justice system. Research concerning individuals' perceptions of and experiences with the police has consistently shown that Black and Hispanic citizens report more distrust and dissatisfaction than their counterparts from other racial groups. Further, the relationship between negative, involuntary law enforcement contacts and citizens' unfavorable evaluations of the police has been well documented. This reader is designed to present a collection of contemporary views and research findings on the topic of racially discriminatory policing practices, and to complement a variety of texts.

RODNEY BRUNSON
University of Alabama at Birmingham

Racially Biased Policing

1

Race and Policing

Jim Leitzel

Police in the United States seem to be doing something right: serious crime has been plummeting, declining by more than 20 percent since 1991. The reduction in the number of murders has been even more spectacular, dropping by more than 36 percent between 1993 and 1999: the murder rate in 1999 was lower than in every year since 1966. Simultaneously, many public areas have become decidedly more hospitable. Aggressive "quality-of-life" policing, such as that employed in New York City to clean up the subway or rid the city of "squeegeemen," may be partly responsible for both the drop in the crime rate and improvements in public spaces.

These successes, however, are tarnished by ongoing controversy concerning the role of race in policing. Race has been an element in some high-profile incidents, such as the February 1999 killing of unarmed African immigrant Amadou Diallo by four white New York City police officers, or the 1997 police torture of Haitian immigrant Abner Louima. But the racial disparities in policing appear to go well beyond isolated cases of abuse. Generally speaking, black people, particularly young black males, tend to have much worse experiences with the police than do white Americans. These experiences range from the annoying—frequent traffic stops for minor or imagined violations—to the fatal, as in the Diallo case. To some extent, racial disparities in citizen-police interactions are deliberate, as criminal "profiles" compiled by the police formally or informally employ race as one factor in identifying potential miscreants. In practice, race appears often to be a decisive element in whether a stop is initiated, or in how an encounter is handled.

Given the success evidenced by falling crime rates, it might be thought that the way forward in crime control is to continue with present policing strategies, while redoubling efforts to eliminate the abuses of racist and brutal

"Race and Policing," by Jim Leitzel from *Society*, Vol. 38, No. 3, March/April 2001, pp. 38–42. Reprinted by permission of Springer.

police. Surely there is wide consensus that such bad cops should be rooted out and prosecuted for their misdeeds. But it is the use of racial profiling, not its abuse, that is the more fundamental problem: even if all abuses associated with race-based policing could somehow be eliminated, racial profiling would remain a bad idea. Race-based policing is counterproductive: it leads to more crime, not less.

IS THERE RACE-BASED POLICING IN THE US?

Perhaps the characterization of racial disparities in policing as a problem is itself misguided. Perhaps there are no actual racial disproportions in police-citizen encounters; or, if disparities do exist, they are a necessary evil, the price that has to be paid for a well-policed society.

Do disparities exist? With respect to traffic regulations, for instance, are blacks and other minorities stopped more frequently, for a given level of violations of the law? Statistics on race, age, sex, and other information from traffic stops are not routinely collected. But information that is available suggests wide racial disparities. The Maryland State Police, in settling a lawsuit, agreed to collect racial information on traffic stops. On Interstate 95, 70 percent of the drivers who were stopped by the state police between January 1995 and December 1997 were African Americans, though African Americans comprised only some 17.5 percent of the drivers (and of the speeding drivers). Videotapes of stops for drug interdiction in Volusia County, Florida, also on I-95, indicated that blacks comprised 5 percent of the drivers, but 70 percent of those who were stopped. Other statistics suggest that the war on drugs is waged primarily against the non-white segment of the population. According to a report written by David Harris for the American Civil Liberties Union (ACLU), "Today, blacks constitute 13 percent of the country's drug users; 37 percent of those arrested on drug charges; 55 percent of those convicted; and 74 percent of all drug offenders sentenced to prison."

Racial disparities in policing exist; indeed, it would be surprising if they did not exist, since race is used as one of the indicators in criminal profiling. Are such disparities understandable, the result of scrupulous policing? While young black males are treated with more suspicion by the police it might be argued that this is natural, because young black males cause a disproportionate amount of trouble. When attempting to prevent or solve street crime, police shouldn't devote much time to tailing elderly women (except perhaps as potential victims of crime)—young males are the likely perpetrators. Conscientious, unbiased policing would seem to require that police focus their suspicions on the most probable threats. By this reckoning, young black males should have more frequent and maybe even less pleasant police encounters than does the rest of the population.

As a seeming bolster to the notion that race-based policing is essential, an appeal might be made to the behavior of private citizens, as opposed to the police. When walking alone down the street at night, suddenly you notice some individuals walking toward you. If you perceive them as a threat, you may want to quickly take evasive action, such as crossing the street or returning to some more populated area. But you only have a few seconds in which to make this decision. The only basis that you have for choosing your route is the small amount of information that you can visually gather, and your prior beliefs about likely and unlikely perpetrators. In a quick glance, you can only learn a few basic facts: the number of individuals, perhaps their size, their sex, and roughly, their age, their manner of dress, and their general comportment. If the strangers are two elderly women, you continue on your way, rightly confident that you are not about to become a crime victim, if they are two young adult males, you might implement your evasion plan. You might be even more likely to take evasive action if it is two black males. You would not be alone in such a reaction: Rev. Jesse Jackson notably mentioned back in 1993 his own pain at subconsciously associating blackness with potential criminality in street encounters.

Private behavior, in making judgments about potential criminality, discriminates on the basis of sex, age, race, and other factors. It seems unavoidable that when better information is not available—and in a chance meeting in the street, only a few characteristics will be observable—group reputations, even if mistaken, play a dominant role in determining private actions. And group reputations can quite easily be mistaken. Few of us actually know how much more likely it is that we will be victimized by a black man than a white man, if indeed it is more likely—most crime involves victims and perpetrators of the same race. Nor would knowledge of crime statistics necessarily resolve the issue. If the police focus their crime-fighting resources on young black men, they will end up arresting such suspects more often than others, even if there is no sex or race based differential in the actual amount of crime. Group reputations for criminality might then yield the appearance of validity, even when they are actually mistaken.

Nevertheless, young men on average are widely believed to be more inclined to predatory violence than elderly women, and without better information, many people will respond to this perception. Such private actions based on group reputation by people who are not racist cannot simply be condemned as inappropriate. In the words of Harvard Law professor Randall Kennedy (whose overall approach to race-based policing is closely paralleled here), those who legally employ race as a signal of potential criminality, "like everyone, are caught up in a large tragedy that will require more than individual good will and bravery to resolve."

Should good cops, then, behave as good private citizens often do? Perhaps surprisingly, the answer is: no. Police should, in general, not use race as a basis for deciding whom to watch, or, after a crime has been committed, whom to question or arrest on grounds of suspicion. This conclusion is not driven by some philosophical perspective that places a higher weight on racial equality than on crime control. Just the opposite: it derives solely from a concern with crime. As in many other policy arenas, the best long-term approach to crime control appears counterproductive in the short-run.

COSTS OF RACE-BASED POLICING

Effective crime control in a democracy requires voluntary cooperation between the police and the citizenry. Voluntary cooperation requires trust. Race-based policing undermines trust. Reduced trust means lessened deterrence of crime, as minorities become unwilling to report crime—a not insignificant concern, given that approximately one-half of serious crime in the United States is not reported to the police. Further, hostility between minorities and the police creates an unwillingness to testify at trials, and, when serving on juries, an unwillingness to convict defendants. This lack of cooperation, brought on by racial disparities in policing, reduces criminal deterrence.

Beyond lowering deterrence, race-based policing also provides positive inducements to disobey the law. When all young black males are thought to be and treated as criminals, a law-abiding black male cannot easily overcome this perception through his own virtuous behavior. Being thought a scoundrel in any event, the reward to virtue falls. The perception of criminality that is inherent in race-based policing prevents well behaving minority youths from distinguishing themselves from those who are criminals, reducing the incentive to be law-abiding.

The problem is not bad or racist cops in an otherwise workable system. Rather, the problem is the hostility and distrust created among police and minority citizens. This pool of hostility between a group of citizens and the police is not the work of a single cop—especially a single good cop—or based on the activities of a single day. Rather, the pool of hostility is created by long-term, numerous interactions between the police and the citizenry. The activities of any single cop over a short period are essentially irrelevant in determining the size of the hostility "pool": they are literally a drop in the ocean. So when a conscientious police officer is doing his (or her) job, he ignores the effect that his actions have on the sea of hostility, because his actions make no noticeable difference. But the sea of hostility is in fact made up of unpleasant police-citizen encounters in the aggregate, despite the fact that any individual encounter, short of an obviously abusive encounter, is of little or no consequence.

Conscientious policing as described above may not only lead to a general mistrust of the police within a minority community, it also can hold rather severe adverse consequences for specific individuals. Police officers who use race and other noisy indicators unrelated to behavior in profiling potential criminals might "rationally" ignore the fact that the same indicators that lead them to make a stop will also lead other officers to do so, too. Thus their stop is often far from an isolated event for the individual in question, but just one in a continuing series of stops, as the famous "San Diego walker" case (Kolender v. Lawson 461 U.S. 352 (1983)) demonstrated. Further, police actions to some extent serve as guides for the behavior of citizens. When private citizens see or learn about racial profiling by police, their own attitudes toward and treatment of minorities are likely to be influenced.

Race-based practices also harm police, even beyond the mistrust that such practices engender. While race-based policing makes it hard for law-abiding young minority males to distinguish themselves from lawbreakers, it simultaneously leads to a parallel stereotyping of police. Race-based policing generates an unfair perception that many or most police officers are at best insensitive to the concerns of minorities or, at worst, racists. So good and honest cops also pay a price for the countenancing of race-based policing, as they become perceived as rough equivalents to those few police whose motivations and acts actually are racist.

Race-based policing presents a familiar scenario, where rational individual behavior does not serve the social good. National defense, the paradigmatic "public good," provides an analogy. Whether or not a particular individual pays his or her taxes has essentially no influence upon the amount of government military spending. Nevertheless, the amount spent on national defense depends on the aggregate amount of taxes paid. If tax payments were voluntary, we would expect too little defense to be supplied: people would recognize that their individual contribution would essentially not matter for the amount of defense provided to them, so they might as well not contribute. Unconstrained individual incentives do not serve society's interests with respect to public goods. Taxes, therefore, are not voluntary. Similarly, citizen hostility toward the police is a "public bad," and individual police officers, acting rationally, will create or "supply" too much of it in the aggregate. Unconstrained individual incentives do not serve society's interests with respect to public bads, either.

AN IMPERFECT SOLUTION

The remedy to the distorted individual incentives that characterize race-based policing is the same as with taxes: we must not allow the use of race in policing to be voluntary. A stringent ban on race-based policing must be adopted. The operational rule of thumb for police officers who are considering stopping or searching a black person (or potentially a Latino or another minority) should be: would I stop or search this person if he or she was white? If the answer is no, then the black person should not be stopped or searched, either, even if, for instance, the neighborhood is predominately white and blacks stopped in the area have been associated with crime in the past. Police "profiles" of drug couriers or other classes of criminals should not include race, even (as is currently done) as one of a panoply of characteristics.

If a description of a suspect is available, race should then be taken into account in attempting to apprehend the suspect. Even here, however, police must be careful to prevent using a description that includes race to cast too wide a net, or as a pretext for a stop unrelated to the crime for which the description was secured.

Important questions remain about how to enforce a ban on race-based policing, and enforcement surely will be imperfect. But the current federal standard, which allows the police to use race not in isolation, but as one of several factors that determine their profiling of potential criminals, is likewise hard to enforce. In fact, evasion of the current standard cannot be prevented, as it is a simple matter to fabricate other, non-race-based factors to accompany race as rationales for police stops or searches. Perhaps the ban on race-based policing will also be easily evaded. But over time, if good police sincerely adopt it, the rule can alter the behavior of all officers, and reduce the pool of hostility towards the police that now exists among many black Americans.

Because using racial indicators of potential criminality appears to be a rational approach for individual police officers (as for private citizens), a conscientious police officer who currently engages in raced-based policing is likely to believe that he or she is doing the right thing, something socially desirable. Adoption of formal rules prohibiting race-based policing will at least make it clear that society does not share that judgment. Race-based activity by police, then, can no longer serve as an open source of pride in a job well done, and this too can reduce the extent of race-based policing over time, even if the prohibition is hard to enforce.

Not all disparities in police-citizen encounters will be eliminated when race-based policing is no longer countenanced: policing high crime areas might require more stops than in other neighborhoods, for instance, and minorities are more likely to live in such neighborhoods. But minorities will also be the beneficiaries of this increased scrutiny, which will be more acceptable when it is not part of an explicit or implicit race-based policing strategy.

Outlawing race-based policing may require other changes. Possibly it might mean an increase in the number of police officers that are required to guard some neighborhoods. It may also mean stopping more citizens in the aggregate, encompassing a broader range than those who are habitually stopped today. (Professor Randall Kennedy discussed these alternatives more fully in his presentation to the National Institute of Justice.) This latter measure would spread more widely the costs imposed by policing, and should not be viewed as necessarily a bad thing. It is easy to support certain laws and police practices if you are unlikely to be burdened by them. But will support for the many searches that take place in the name of the war on drugs, for instance, survive a broadening of the citizenry that is subject to such searches? A rule prohibiting race-based policing will not only serve the long-run goal of controlling crime, but will also help to protect, for all citizens, constitutionally guaranteed rights against illegal search and seizure. One area in which a prohibition on race-based policing might require supplementary measures is in traffic patrolling. The complexity of traffic laws guarantees available pretexts for race-based stops, and as a result, differential traffic stops occasioned by race-based policing currently appear to be widespread. But as traffic stops are more formal than street-to-street encounters (and typically constrained to take place within a short distance of the patrol car), they can be more closely monitored. Videotaping stops (which already occurs in some jurisdictions), and the collection of statistics on the race of stopped drivers (which is now done by law in some states by executive order for federal law enforcers, and voluntarily by other police departments), offer means to ensure that strictures against race-based policing are not ignored.

The formal repudiation of race-based policing can be complemented with a strategy to enforce strict limits on the actions that the state can take in the absence of more compelling evidence of wrongdoing than noisy signals like gender, race, and age. In the drug search example, for instance, the searches can be limited to be of only a few minutes duration, and restrictions can be placed on the extent of their intrusiveness. Whether race-based policing is countenanced or not, there must be strict ceilings to what actions the state can take in the absence of information more incriminating than "suspicion" or group reputation. Otherwise, outrages such as the US internment of Japanese-Americans during World War II, or the mundane, daily outrages that some members of targeted groups are subjected to by police, will continue to be repeated.

In the long run, there is no trade-off between crime control and race-neutral policing: more of one does not mean less of the other. Indeed, just the opposite. But the immediate rejection of race-based policing will not immediately reduce distrust between police and minority communities. The distrust has been fostered over many years, and it will take sustained changes in police policy and behavior to reduce the sea of hostility. The time to make the change to race-neutral policing, then, is when crime is relatively low. What the police have been doing right has helped to bring about the low crime rates that we currently enjoy. We should take advantage of these low crime rates to change, now, what the police, generally in good faith, have been doing wrong.

Jim Leitzel *is senior lecturer in the Social Sciences Collegiate Division, University of Chicago.*

SUGGESTED FURTHER READINGS

Cole, David. No Equal Justice: Race and Class in the American Criminal Justice System. New York: The New Press, 1999.

Davis, Marcia. "Traffic Violation: Racial Profiling Is a Reality for Black Drivers." Emerge, pp. 42–48, June 1999.

Harris, David. "Driving While Black: Racial Profiling on Our Nation's Highways." American Civil Liberties Union Special Report, June 1999, available at www.aclu.org/profiling/report/index.html.

Kennedy, Randall. Race, Crime, and the Law. New York: Random House, 1997.

Merida, Kevin. "Capital Scene: Decriminalizing 'Driving While Black.'" Emerge, p. 26, December/January 1999.

Kennedy, Randall. "Race, the Police, and 'Reasonable Suspicion'?" Presentation to the National Institute of Justice, February 3, 1998. Perspectives on Crime and Justice: 1997–1998 Lecture Series, available at www.ojp.usdoj.gov/nij/pubs-sum/172851.htm.

2

Racially Biased Policing: Determinants of Citizen Perceptions*

Ronald Weitzer and Steven A. Tuch

The current controversy surrounding racial profiling in America has focused renewed attention on the larger issue of racial bias by the police. Yet little is known about the extent of police racial bias and even less about public perceptions of the problem. This article analyzes recent national survey data on citizens' views of, and reported personal experiences with, several forms of police bias—including differential treatment of individuals and neighborhoods, police prejudice, and racial profiling. We find that attitudes toward the prevalence and acceptability of these practices are largely shaped by citizens' race, personal experiences with police discrimination, and exposure to news media reporting on incidents of police misconduct. The findings lend support to the group-position theory of race relations.

Racial bias by the police includes such things as racial profiling of motorists, racial prejudice among police officers, and discriminatory treatment of minority individuals and minority neighborhoods. Little research exists on public perceptions of racially biased policing, though such perceptions may have important consequences. The perception of police practices as unfair or as racially motivated may lead to more frequent and severe confrontations between police and citizens and to greater distrust of the police. This article examines citizens' views of and reported experiences with police bias and the major determinants of citizens' perceptions.

"Racially Biased Policing: Determinants of Citizen Perceptions," by Ronald Weitzer and Steven A. Tuch from *Social Forces,* Volume 83, No. 3, pp. 1009–1030. Copyright © 2005 by the University of North Carolina Press. Used by permission of the publisher, www.uncpress.unc.edu.

EXPLAINING PUBLIC PERCEPTIONS
OF THE POLICE

Race is one of the most consistent predictors of attitudes toward the police. African Americans are significantly more likely than whites to hold negative views of the police, but very little is known about Hispanics' views. Do Hispanics tend to take a "minority group" perspective similar to that of African Americans; do they take an intermediate position in a white-Hispanic-black "racial hierarchy" pattern; or are their views more closely aligned with those of whites? Since only a few studies systematically compare police relations with Hispanics, blacks, and whites, the literature is insufficient to address these questions.

A larger deficiency in the empirical literature concerns the question of why racial differences exist in citizens' relations with the police. We argue that part of the explanation can be found in the group-position thesis, a variant of conflict theory. The group-position thesis focuses on intergroup competition over material rewards, status, and power. Racial attitudes reflect not merely individual-level feelings and beliefs but also a collective "sense of group position" vis-a-vis other racial groups (Blumer 1958), including (1) perceived threats: dominant group members' fears that their group is at risk of losing privileges or resources to competing racial groups, and (2) perceived advantages: minority group members' beliefs that their group interests will be enhanced by challenging the prevailing racial order.

The group-position thesis has been used to explain intergroup racial attitudes (Blumer 1958; Bobo and Hutchings 1996; Kinder and Sanders 1996); we extend it to an analysis of group relations with social institutions. If the dominant group believes that it is entitled to valuable resources, it follows that the group will have an affinity with the institutions that serve their interests. One such institution is the criminal justice system.

Dominant racial groups typically see the police as allies. This is especially transparent in deeply divided societies, like Northern Ireland and South Africa, where the police are or were a key institutional pillar in a sectarian sociopolitical system, and where the dominant racial or ethnic group traditionally views the police as an instrument for suppressing subordinate groups (Weitzer 1995). This affinity between the police and dominant groups is less pronounced in more democratic societies, but we argue that even in these societies, the general group-position dynamic structures group relations with the police. In the U.S., white support for the police has traditionally been robust. At the same time, whites tend to see blacks as inclined to criminal or violent behavior (Hurwitz and Peffley 1997). In the 2000 General Social Survey, for example, half of whites viewed blacks as "violence-prone." For whites who subscribe to these views, there is a tendency to condone police suspicion and disparate treatment of blacks as "rational discrimination" (Weitzer 2000). These attitudes may be more strongly held by some whites (the most racially prejudiced) than by others (Cohn and Barkan 2004), but the group-position thesis predicts that these views are fairly common throughout the white population. Thus, for many whites, it seems sensible for law enforcement to target minority individuals or minority neighborhoods.

If whites tend to align themselves with the police, it follows that, when the police are criticized, whites may perceive their group interests as indirectly threatened (Bayley and Mendelsohn 1969; Jackson 1989). Our extension of group-position theory predicts that whites will tend to be dubious or dismissive of allegations of police misconduct. To accept that minorities are frequently mistreated would lend credence to reforms—reforms that might dilute crime control, thereby threatening whites. African Americans and Hispanics, on the other hand, should be more inclined to view the police as engaged in frequent abuse of minority citizens and, thus, as a "visible sign of majority domination" (Bayley and Mendelsohn 1969:195). This view of police does not mean that minorities are monolithically critical of the police, but it does increase the chances that they will see police misconduct as both a general problem and one that particularly afflicts Hispanics and blacks (Weitzer and Tuch 2004a).

The group-position thesis stresses perceived (not necessarily real) threats to dominant group interests (Bobo and Hutchings 1996; Kinder and Sanders 1996). While most blacks and Hispanics want more law enforcement, (1) leaders within the minority community often criticize the police in public, which may reinforce whites' impressions that minorities are trying to interfere with crime control. In a nutshell, white skepticism of charges of police wrongdoing may be partly rooted in their attachment to the law-and-order status quo; minority perceptions of misconduct, on the other hand, may reflect their desire to gain better treatment from the police.

Although we do not have direct measures of group interests and threats, our data do allow us to test the key predictions of group-position theory—namely, white defense of the police against charges of racial discrimination and minority belief that police racial bias is a serious problem. As noted above, it is unclear from the literature whether blacks and Hispanics hold roughly similar views or whether one group is more critical of the police. But just as African Americans have a deeper and more crystallized sense of relative group position vis-a-vis whites than is true for Hispanics (Bobo 1999), they also have a longer and more fractious history with the police in America. This is one reason that blacks' opinions of the police might be expected to be significantly more negative than Hispanics'. Again, we lack a critical mass of studies on this issue.

Most of the literature is exclusively centered on the role of demographic characteristics in shaping views of the police (Brown and Benedict 2002; Gallagher et al. 2001; Weitzer and Tuch 1999). The role of nondemographic factors—both micro and macro—remains unclear. This is particularly true for "the public's personal experiences with the police, what they learn second-hand from friends and acquaintances, and what they learn from the media" (Gallagher et al. 2001:v). A few studies suggest that these experiential and media factors may influence attitudes. Citizens' personal contacts with the police—especially negative experiences—appear to influence citizens' larger views of the police (Tyler and Huo 2002). One's personal contacts thus seem to affect how people view the police more generally. Moreover, it is also possible that the experiences of family members and friends may be internalized and "vicariously experienced" by the actor, affecting his or her larger views of the police. Similarly, exposure to media reports on incidents of police misconduct (e.g., Rodney King) may adversely affect citizens' confidence in the police, and this effect may be especially true for members of minority groups (Kaminski and Jefferis 1998; Sigelman et al. 1997; Tuch and Weitzer 1997; Weitzer 2002). But much more research is necessary to test these predictions. The present study examines whether citizens' views of racially biased policing are shaped by citizens' personal experiences, knowledge of others' experiences, and exposure to media reporting on the police—and whether the effects of these factors are more cogent among blacks and Hispanics than among whites.

We test the following hypotheses:

Hypothesis 1a: Blacks and Hispanics are more likely than whites to believe that various forms of racially biased policing exist.

Hypothesis 1b: These racial differences persist net of the influences of experiential, media, and control variables.

Hypothesis 2a: Exposure to media reports of police misconduct increases perceptions of police bias among all groups.

Hypothesis 2b: The effect, however, is stronger for blacks and Hispanics than for whites.

Hypothesis 3a: Personal or vicarious experience with police bias increases perceptions of bias among all groups.

Hypothesis 3b: The effect, however, is stronger for blacks and Hispanics than for whites.

DATA AND METHODS

Data for this study come from the authors' 2002 national survey of 1,792 white, African American, and Hispanic adult residents of U.S. metropolitan areas with at least 100,000 population. The sample is representative of adults living in households with telephones in urban and suburban areas that meet this population-size criterion.

The data for this article were collected as part of a larger study by the authors of police-citizen relations in the U.S. The survey has the advantages of (1) oversampling African Americans and Hispanics, in contrast to the small number of minority respondents typically included in other surveys, and (2) tapping both attitudes toward police and personal and vicarious experiences with the police.

SAMPLING

The survey was conducted for the authors by Knowledge Networks, a Web-based survey research firm that combines probability sampling with the reach and capabilities of the Internet to yield representative samples of respondents without sacrificing data quality. Research comparing the quality of data yielded by Knowledge Networks' Web-based survey methodology with that of random-digit dialing telephone surveys has found that Knowledge Networks yields representative samples that produce parameter estimates very similar to the estimates of random-digit dialing samples (Baker et al. 2003; Berrens 2003; Krosnick and Chang 2001).

Knowledge Networks uses list-assisted random-digit dialing sampling techniques on a sample frame consisting of the entire telephone population, so that any household with a telephone can be selected for the Knowledge Networks panel, including computer users and nonusers alike. In exchange for free Internet hardware (such as a television set-top box), connectivity (an Internet connection paid for by Knowledge Networks), and on-site installation, participants agree to complete a maximum of three to four surveys per month. Selected households remain on the panel for two to three years. Currently, Knowledge Networks has more than 25,000 households in its Web-enabled panel.

PANEL REPRESENTATIVENESS

When using panels for survey research, potential sampling bias can occur at any of several stages. First, respondents consent to become panel members; this is referred to as the panel acceptance rate. At the time of the study, Knowledge Networks panel acceptance rate was 40%, calculated by standards established by the American Association for Public Opinion Research. (2) Second, the within-survey completion rate—or percentage of panel members who completed our questionnaire among those who received it—was 67%.

The Knowledge Networks panel is representative of and closely mirrors the U.S. population on key demographic, geographic, economic, and social characteristics. Four factors account for this representativeness. First, as mentioned above, the panel is selected using random-digit dialing telephone methodology, providing a probability-based starting sample of telephone households (according to the census, 98% of white households, 95% of Hispanic households, and 94% of African American households have telephone access). Second, the panel weights are adjusted to census demographic benchmarks to reduce error due to noncoverage of households without telephones and to reduce bias due to nonresponse and other nonsampling errors. Third, samples selected from the panel for individual studies are selected by probability methods, and sample design weights for each study are calculated to meet the design parameters. Fourth, nonresponse and poststratification weighting adjustments are applied to the final survey data to reduce the effects of nonsampling error. The result is that the weighted demographic estimates from the census and the Knowledge Networks panel differ very little across gender, age, race/ethnicity, education, and region (see Table 1 for descriptive sample statistics). Moreover, analyses of panel attrition indicate that no significant differences separate those who remain on the panel from those who do not (Dennis and Li 2003). (3)

TABLE 1   Descriptive Statistics: Means (and Standard Deviations) on All Variables

Total Sample

Education	4.06 (1.68)
Income	9.94 (3.95)
Gender (1 = male)	.49 (.50)
Age	45.40 (16.74)
Residence (1 = city)	.70 (.46)
Region (1 = south)	.35 (.48)
Safety (day)	1.36 (.61)
Safety (night)	1.77 (.80)
Neighborhood crime	1.96 (.78)
Media exposure	2.97 (.73)
Personal experience (1 = yes)	.15 (.36)
Vicarious experience (1 = yes)	.13 (.34)
Bias against individuals	5.19 (1.75)
Bias against neighborhoods	2.77 (1.12)
Police prejudice	7.68 (2.47)
Racial profiling	3.16 (1.82)

Whites

Education	4.18 (1.69) (a,b)
Income	10.34 (3.70) (a,b)
Gender (1 = male)	.50 (.50) (a)
Age	47.43 (16.93) (a,b)
Residence (1 = city)	.65 (.48) (a,b)
Region (1 = south)	.32 (.47) (a)
Safety (day)	1.26 (.55) (a,b)
Safety (night)	1.66 (.75) (a,b)
Neighborhood crime	1.84 (.72) (a,b)
Media exposure	2.89 (.68) (a,b)

TABLE 1 *Continued*

Whites

Personal experience (1 = yes)	.05 (.22) (a,b)
Vicarious experience (1 = yes)	.05 (.22) (a,b)
Bias against individuals	4.70 (1.42) (a,b)
Bias against neighborhoods	2.55 (1.09) (a,b)
Police prejudice	7.03 (2.19) (a,b)
Racial profiling	2.67 (1.63) (a,b)

Blacks

Education	3.72 (1.52) (a,c)
Income	8.59 (4.12) (a)
Gender (1 = male)	.44 (.50) (a)
Age	40.49 (15.52) (a,c)
Residence (1 = city)	.70 (.46) (a,c)
Region (1 = south)	.51 (.50) (a,c)
Safety (day)	1.56 (.68) (a)
Safety (night)	2.00 (.85) (a)
Neighborhood crime	2.27 (.86) (a)
Media exposure	3.25 (.79) (a,c)
Personal experience (1 = yes)	.50 (.50) (a,c)
Vicarious experience (1 = yes)	.38 (.49) (a,c)
Bias against individuals	6.59 (1.85) (a,c)
Bias against neighborhoods	3.44 (.94) (a,c)
Police prejudice	9.69 (2.17) (a,c)
Racial profiling	4.75 (1.46)

Hispanics

Education	3.33 (1.59) (b,c)
Income	8.86 (4.14) (b)
Gender (1 = male)	.49 (.50)
Age	37.43 (14.39) (b,c)
Residence (1 = city)	.79 (.41) (b,c)
Region (1 = south)	.28 (.45) (c)
Safety (day)	1.63 (.77) (b)
Safety (night)	2.06 (.92) (b)
Neighborhood crime	2.19 (.88) (b)
Media exposure	3.07 (.80) (b,c)
Personal experience (1 = yes)	.32 (.47) (b,c)
Vicarious experience (1 = yes)	.30 (.46) (b,c)
Bias against individuals	5.94 (2.02) (b,c)
Bias against neighborhoods	3.16 (1.03) (b,c)
Police prejudice	8.78 (2.49) (b,c)
Racial profiling	3.99 (1.78) (b,c)

(a) The white and black means are significantly different, p < .05.
(b) The white and Hispanic means are significantly different, p < .05.
(c) The black and Hispanic means are significantly different, p < .05.

INDEPENDENT VARIABLES

Race

We use the term "race" broadly to include both racial and ethnic groups. Our sample consists of respondents who self-identify as African American, Hispanic, or non-Hispanic white on Knowledge Networks demographic profile of panel members.

Experiences with Police Discrimination

Perceived personal and vicarious experiences with discriminatory police behavior were measured with the following questions: "Have you ever felt that you were treated unfairly by the police specifically because of your race in [your city/your own neighborhood]?" "Have you ever felt that you were stopped by the police just because of your race or ethnic background?" Parallel questions tapped vicarious experience, with reference to whether this had happened to anyone else in the respondent's household. (4) Responses to the personal experience questions were combined to form an index of reported personal experience with police bias; responses to the vicarious experience questions were combined to create an index of reported vicarious experience with police bias. The alpha reliability coefficient is .80 for the personal experience index and .84 for the vicarious index. In the analysis, both indices are dichotomized (1 = experience with bias, 0 = no experience).

Media Exposure

We asked the following question in order to gauge respondents' exposure to media accounts of police misconduct: "How often do you hear or read about (on the radio, television, or in the newspapers) incidents of police misconduct (such as police use of excessive force, verbal abuse, and corruption) that occur somewhere in the nation?" Response options were "never," "rarely," "sometimes," and "often" on a four-point scale coded so that higher scores indicate more frequent exposure. (5)

Controls

We control on several demographic factors: age, in years; gender (1 = male, 0 = female); place of residence, measured with a dummy variable for city (coded 1) versus suburb (coded 0); region (1 = south, 0 = nonsouth); education, measured on a 9-point ladder ranging from less than high school (coded 1) to doctorate degree (coded 9); and household income, measured on a 17-step ladder ranging from less than $5,000 per year (coded 1) to $125,000 or more (coded 17). Three items measure respondents' assessment of neighborhood crime conditions: "Overall, how safe do you feel being alone outside in your neighborhood [during the day/at night]—very safe, somewhat safe, somewhat unsafe, or very unsafe?" "How serious a problem is crime in your neighborhood—very serious, somewhat serious, not serious, or not a problem at all?" Responses to these questions are coded so that higher scores reflect less safety and more perceived neighborhood crime.

DEPENDENT VARIABLES

Perceptions of police racial bias (6) were measured by four sets of questions, with each set of items combined into a scale: (1) Racial bias against individuals: "Do you think the police in your [city/neighborhood] treat whites and blacks equally, do they treat whites worse than blacks, or blacks worse than whites?" A parallel question asked respondents to compare whites and Hispanics. Alpha for this index is .91. (2) Racial bias against neighborhoods: The police engage in positive and negative typifications of different locales (Smith 1986), which may lead to disparate treatment of neighborhoods. We asked, "In general in the U.S., do you think that police services in white neighborhoods are better, worse, or about the same as in black neighborhoods?" A parallel question asked for a comparison between white and Hispanic neighborhoods. Alpha for this index is .88. (3) Police prejudice: "How common do you think racial or ethnic prejudice is among police officers [throughout the U.S./in your city/in your neighborhood]?" Alpha for this index is .86. (4) Racial profiling: "Since many drivers engage in minor traffic violations like speeding, it is sometimes hard to tell why some drivers get stopped by the police while others do not. Do you think that black drivers are more likely to be stopped by the police than white drivers for the same types of violations?" A parallel question compared Hispanic and white drivers. Regarding approval of profiling, we replicated a 1999 Gallup poll question: "There have been reports that some police officers stop drivers from certain racial groups because they think members of these groups are more likely to commit crimes. This is known as 'racial profiling.' Do you approve or disapprove of the use of this practice?" Regarding the scope of profiling, we asked, "Do you think that racial profiling is widespread or not widespread [in the U.S./in your city/in your neighborhood]?" Alpha for the profiling index is .73.

Table 1 presents descriptive statistics for all study variables. Compared to whites, African Americans and Hispanics in our sample report significantly less education and lower incomes; are younger; reside in cities rather than suburbs; report less neighborhood safety and more crime; report greater exposure to media coverage of police misconduct; and have more frequent experiences with, and greater perceptions of, police bias. Blacks and Hispanics also differ significantly on each of these variables (except income, neighborhood safety, and crime). Blacks are more likely than Hispanics to report media exposure to police misconduct and personal/vicarious experience with racially biased policing, and they are also more likely to perceive the existence of our four types of police racial bias.

Results

Hypothesis 1 predicted that blacks and Hispanics are more likely than whites to believe that racially biased policing exists. To test this hypothesis, we first cross-tabulated with race each of the items that compose the various racial bias indices; we briefly summarize those results here (not shown in a table). First, a majority of blacks (75%) and Hispanics (54%) believe that police in their city treat blacks worse than whites, and virtually the same proportions also believe that Hispanics are treated worse than whites (74% and 53%, respectively). Few whites agree: The overwhelming majority of whites (75%–77%) believe that police in their city treat whites and the two minority groups "equally." (7)

A second set of questions pertains to perceived disparities in police services toward neighborhoods populated by the racial groups. A majority of blacks and Hispanics—but just one-third of whites—believes that police provide "worse" services to black and Hispanic neighborhoods (in comparison to white neighborhoods) throughout the U.S. It is interesting that blacks are more likely than Hispanics (77% vs. 61%, respectively) to believe that Hispanic neighborhoods are treated worse than white areas. The majority of whites believe that police treat neighborhoods similarly.

Third, blacks and Hispanics are also much more likely than whites to believe that police prejudice is a problem. Three times as many blacks as whites believe that police prejudice is "very common" throughout the U.S., and blacks are about six times as likely as whites to believe it is very common in their own city (Hispanics take an intermediate position). And fourth, while large majorities of all three groups disapprove of racial profiling (73% of whites, 77% of Hispanics, 90% of blacks) and believe that it is widespread in the U.S. (70% of whites, 83% of Hispanics, 92% of blacks), only a third of whites believe that profiling is pervasive in their own city (vs. 59% of Hispanics and 80% of blacks).

Finally, a large gulf separates minorities and whites when it comes to their own experiences with racial discrimination by the police. For instance, significant numbers of Hispanics (23%) and blacks (37%), but almost no whites (1%), report being "treated unfairly" by police in their city specifically because of their race, and similar percentages of each group report being stopped by police solely because of their race. The same disparities are found for vicarious experience, that is, racially biased treatment of someone in the respondent's household.

These race differences are consistent with hypothesis 1a, but do they persist net of the influences of demographic, neighborhood, media, and experiential variables? And what other factors besides race shape views of police bias? To answer these questions, we turn to the multivariate results in Table 2.

Table 2 displays results from regressing each of the police bias indices on race, the other demographics, and the neighborhood, media, and experience variables. Each model in the table presents coefficients both for the total sample

TABLE 2 OLS Estimates for the Regression of Perceived Police Bias on Predictors (a)

Model 1. Bias against Individuals

	Total Sample	
	b	**beta**
Demographics		
Black	1.170 ★★★	.233
	(.127)	
Hispanic	.704 ★★★	.145
	(.114)	
Education	.120 ★★★	.116
	(.024)	
Income	−.005	−.011
	(.010)	
Gender (1 = male)	.097	.028
	(.075)	
Age	−.006 ★★	−.058
	(.002)	
Residence (1 = city)	.231 ★★	.061
	(.081)	
Region (1 = south)	.029	.008
	(.079)	
Neighborhood		
Safety (day)	.145	.049
	(.089)	
Safety (night)	.018	.008
	(.068)	
Neighborhood crime	.142 ★★	.062
	(.056)	
Policing		
Media exposure	.451 ★★★	.186
	(.053)	
Personal experience (1 = yes)	.823 ★★★	.168
	(.133)	
Vicarious experience (1 = yes)	.207	.040
	(.136)	
Constant	2.529	
Adjusted R^2	.273	
N of cases (unweighted)	1,521	

	Whites	
	b	**beta**
Demographics		
Black	—	—
Hispanic	—	—

Continued

TABLE 2 *Continued*

	Whites	
	b	**beta**
Education	.139 ★★★	.167
	(.037)	
Income	−.022	−.056
	(.017)	
Gender (1 = male)	.191	.067
	(.118)	
Age	−.008 ★	−.096
	(.004)	
Residence (1 = city)	.281 ★	.095
	(.119)	
Region (1 = south)	.104	.034
	(.123)	
Neighborhood		
Safety (day)	.164	.057
	(.153)	
Safety (night)	.084	.042
	(.090)	
Neighborhood crime	.008	.004
	(.090)	
Policing		
Media exposure	.478 ★★★	.225
	(.087)	
Personal experience (1 = yes)	.112 (b,c)	.002
	(.319)	
Vicarious experience (1 = yes)	.157	.022
	.339	
Constant	2.669	
Adjusted R^2	.078	
N of cases (unweighted)	552	

	Blacks	
	b	**beta**
Demographics		
Black	—	—
Hispanic	—	—
Education	.050	.041
	(.055)	
Income	.048 ★★	.109
	(.019)	
Gender (1 = male)	−.279	−.076
	(.164)	
Age	−.007	−.061
	(.005)	

TABLE 2 *Continued*

	Blacks	
	b	**beta**
Residence (1 = city)	.316	.079
	(.178)	
Region (1 = south)	.112	.031
	(.160)	
Neighborhood		
Safety (day)	.452 ★★	.163
	(.167)	
Safety (night)	−.077	−.035
	(.136)	
Neighborhood crime	.261 ★★	.121
	(.101)	
Policing		
Media exposure	.266 ★★	.114
	(.101)	
Personal experience (1 = yes)	1.091 ★★★ (b)	.297
	(.179)	
Vicarious experience (1 = yes)	.161	.043
	(.176)	
Constant	3.568	
Adjusted R^2	.184	
N of cases (unweighted)	454	

	Hispanics	
	b	**beta**
Demographics		
Black	—	—
Hispanic	—	—
Education	.028	.022
	(.053)	
Income	.038	.077
	(.022)	
Gender (1 = male)	.289	.073
	(.166)	
Age	−.007	−.051
	(.006)	
Residence (1 = city)	.130	.027
	(.197)	
Region (1 = south)	.037	.008
	(.181)	
Neighborhood		
Safety (day)	.167	.064
	(.164)	

Continued

TABLE 2 *Continued*

	Hispanics	
	b	beta
Safety (night)	−.047	−.022
	(.141)	
Neighborhood crime	.262 ★	.112
	(.110)	
Policing		
Media exposure	.517 ★★★	.205
	(.105)	
Personal experience (1 = yes)	1.396 ★★★ (c)	.326
	(.198)	
Vicarious experience (1 = yes)	.170	.038
	(.197)	
Constant	2.706	
Adjusted R^2	.223	
N of cases (unweighted)	515	

Model 2. Bias against Neighborhoods

	Total Sample	
	b	beta
Demographics		
Black	.618 ★★★	.193
	(.085)	
Hispanic	.397 ★★★	.128
	(.077)	
Education	.084 ★★★	.127
	(.016)	
Income	−.007	−.023
	(.007)	
Gender (1 = male)	−.034	−.051
	(.050)	
Age	−.005 ★★★	−.080
	(.002)	
Residence (1 = city)	.097	.041
	(.054)	
Region (1 = south)	−.061	−.026
	(.052)	
Neighborhood		
Safety (day)	−.053	−.028
	(.060)	
Safety (night)	.096 ★	.068
	(.045)	
Neighborhood crime	.062	.043
	(.037)	

TABLE 2 *Continued*

	Total Sample	
	b	**beta**
Policing		
Media exposure	.322 ★★★	.208
	(.036)	
Personal experience (1 = yes)	.280 ★★	.089
	(.090)	
Vicarious experience (1 = yes)	.108	.032
	(.091)	
Constant	1.593	
Adjusted R^2	.176	
N of cases (unweighted)	1,550	

	Whites	
	b	**beta**
Demographics		
Black	—	—
Hispanic	—	—
Education	.112 ★★★	.177
	(.028)	
Income	−.022	−.073
	(.013)	
Gender (1 = male)	.057	.026
	(.089)	
Age	−.006 ★	−.092
	(.003)	
Residence (1 = city)	.095	.042
	(.090)	
Region (1 = south)	−.041	−.018
	(.092)	
Neighborhood		
Safety (day)	.069	.032
	(.115)	
Safety (night)	.087	.058
	(.081)	
Neighborhood crime	.151 ★	.100
	(.067)	
Policing		
Media exposure	.332 ★★★	.207
	(.065)	
Personal experience (1 = yes)	.078	.015
	(.247)	

Continued

TABLE 2 *Continued*

	Whites	
	b	**beta**
Vicarious experience (1 = yes)	.344	.063
	(.259)	
Constant	.160	
Adjusted R^2	.065	
N of cases (unweighted)	564	

	Blacks	
	b	**beta**
Demographics		
Black	—	—
Hispanic	—	—
Education	.054 ★	.088
	(.027)	
Income	.036 ★★★	.159
	(.010)	
Gender (1 = male)	−.081	−.044
	(.080)	
Age	−.007 ★★	−.111
	(.002)	
Residence (1 = city)	.098	.049
	(.085)	
Region (1 = south)	−.046	−.025
	(.078)	
Neighborhood		
Safety (day)	−.220 ★★	−.157
	(.081)	
Safety (night)	.174 ★★	.156
	(.066)	
Neighborhood crime	.051	.048
	(.049)	
Policing		
Media exposure	.414 ★★★ (d)	.356
	(.048)	
Personal experience (1 = yes)	.273 ★★	.148
	(.086)	
Vicarious experience (1 = yes)	−.040	−.021
	(.085)	
Constant	1.629	
Adjusted R^2	.228	
N of cases (unweighted)	463	

TABLE 2 *Continued*

	Hispanics	
	b	beta
Demographics		
Black	—	—
Hispanic	—	—
Education	−.036	−.056
	(.028)	
Income	.018	.070
	(.012)	
Gender (1 = male)	−.078 ★	−.087
	(.089)	
Age	−.005	−.073
	(.003)	
Residence (1 = city)	−.003	−.001
	(.106)	
Region (1 = south)	.093	.041
	−.098	
Neighborhood		
Safety (day)	−.277 ★★	−.206
	(.088)	
Safety (night)	.140	.125
	(.076)	
Neighborhood crime	.076	.063
	(.059)	
Policing		
Media exposure	.261 ★★★ (d)	.202
	(.057)	
Personal experience (1 = yes)	.429 ★★★	.196
	(.107)	
Vicarious experience (1 = yes)	.092	.041
	(.104)	
Constant	2.441	
Adjusted R^2	.123	
N of cases (unweighted)	523	

Model 3. Police Prejudice

	Total Sample	
	b	beta
Demographics		
Black	.891 ★★★	.126
	(.163)	
Hispanic	.528 ★★★	.077
	(.148)	

Continued

TABLE 2 *Continued*

	Total Sample	
	b	**beta**
Education	.009	.006
	(.031)	
Income	−.012	−.091
	(.013)	
Gender (1 = male)	−.157	−.032
	(.097)	
Age	−.020 ★★★	−.137
	(.003)	
Residence (1 = city)	.244 ★	.046
	(.104)	
Region (1 = south)	.194	.038
	(.101)	
Neighborhood		
Safety (day)	−.085	−.014
	(.116)	
Safety (night)	.129	.041
	(.087)	
Neighborhood crime	.311 ★★★	.096
	(.072)	
Policing		
Media exposure	.885 ★★★	.259
	(.068)	
Personal experience (1 = yes)	1.685 ★★★	.246
	(.171)	
Vicarious experience (1 = yes)	.793 ★★★	.107
	(.177)	
Constant	4.534	
Adjusted R^2	.383	
N of cases (unweighted)	1,534	

	Whites	
	b	**beta**
Demographics		
Black	—	—
Hispanic	—	—
Education	.018	.014
	(.051)	
Income	−.016	−.027
	(.024)	
Gender (1 = male)	−.149	−.034
	(.164)	

TABLE 2 *Continued*

	Whites	
	b	**beta**
Age	−.026 ★★★	−.201
	(.005)	
Residence (1 = city)	.199	.044
	(.165)	
Region (1 = south)	.224	.048
	(.170)	
Neighborhood		
Safety (day)	.005	.001
	(.213)	
Safety (night)	.168	.054
	(.150)	
Neighborhood crime	.160	.052
	(.124)	
Policing		
Media exposure	.940 ★★★	.291
	(.120)	
Personal experience (1 = yes)	2.089 ★★★	.205
	(.436) ★★★	
Vicarious experience (1 = yes)	.998 ★	.090
	(.478)	
Constant	4.789	
Adjusted R²	.232	
N of cases (unweighted)	555	

	Blacks	
	b	**beta**
Demographics		
Black	—	—
Hispanic	—	—
Education	.009	.006
	(.059)	
Income	−.005	−.010
	(.021)	
Gender (1 = male)	.074	.017
	(.174)	
Age	.001	.002
	(.005)	
Residence (1 = city)	.531 ★★	.113
	(.187)	
Region (1 = south)	.528 ★★	.122
	(.170)	

Continued

TABLE 2 *Continued*

	Blacks	
	b	**beta**
Neighborhood		
Safety (day)	−.229	−.070
	(.177)	
Safety (night)	.247	.095
	(.144)	
Neighborhood crime	.349 ★★★	.139
	(.106)	
Policing		
Media exposure	.721 ★★★	.266
	(.106)	
Personal experience (1 = yes)	1.496 ★★★	.346
	(.189)	
Vicarious experience (1 = yes)	.381 ★ (d)	.086
	(.186)	
Constant	4.851	
Adjusted R^2	.325	
N of cases (unweighted)	463	

	Hispanics	
	b	**beta**
Demographics		
Black	—	—
Hispanic	—	—
Education	.006	.004
	(.061)	
Income	.017	.027
	(.025)	
Gender (1 = male)	−.320	−.065
	(.190)	
Age	−.008	−.046
	(.007)	
Residence (1 = city)	.501 ★	.083
	(.224)	
Region (1 = south)	−.029	−.005
	(.208)	
Neighborhood		
Safety (day)	−.120	−.037
	(.188)	
Safety (night)	−.094	−.035
	(.161)	
Neighborhood crime	.566 ★★★	.193
	(.129)	

TABLE 2 *Continued*

	Hispanics	
	b	beta
Policing		
Media exposure	.742 ★★★	.235
	(.121)	
Personal experience (1 = yes)	1.672 ★★★	.313
	(.229)	
Vicarious experience (1 = yes)	.999 ★★★ (d)	.181
	(.225)	
Constant	4.682	
Adjusted R^2	.344	
N of cases (unweighted)	516	

Model 4. Racial Profiling

	Total Sample	
	b	beta
Demographics		
Black	1.210 ★★★	.230
	(.128)	
Hispanic	.632 ★★★	.124
	(.115)	
Education	.083 ★★★	.077
	(.024)	
Income	−.025 ★	−.054
	(.010)	
Gender (1 = male)	−.029	−.008
	(.076)	
Age	−.014 ★★★	−.125
	(.002)	
Residence (1 = city)	.177 ★	.042
	(.081)	
Region (1 = south)	−.151	−.039
	(.079)	
Neighborhood		
Safety (day)	.083	.013
	(.090)	
Safety (night)	−.054	−.023
	(.068)	
Neighborhood crime	.266 ★★★	.112
	(.056)	
Policing		
Media exposure	.467 ★★★	.184
	(.053)	

Continued

TABLE 2 *Continued*

	Total Sample	
	b	**beta**
Personal experience (1 = yes)	.780 ★★★	.153
	(.133)	
Vicarious experience (1 = yes)	.490 ★★★	.089
	(.138)	
Constant	1.329	
Adjusted R^2	.320	
N of cases (unweighted)	1,526	

	Whites	
	b	**beta**
Demographics		
Black	—	—
Hispanic	—	—
Education	.122 ★★	.127
	(.041)	
Income	−.046 ★	−.103
	(.019)	
Gender (1 = male)	.019	.116
	(.131)	
Age	−.018 ★★★	−.184
	(.004)	
Residence (1 = city)	.118	.035
	(.132)	
Region (1 = south)	−.190	−.055
	(.135)	
Neighborhood		
Safety (day)	.149	.046
	(.168)	
Safety (night)	−.080	−.036
	(.119)	
Neighborhood crime	.192 ★	.084
	(.099)	
Policing		
Media exposure	.504 ★★★	.209
	(.095)	
Personal experience (1 = yes)	.414 (c)	.054
	(.345)	
Vicarious experience (1 = yes)	.914 ★	.112
	(.374)	
Constant	1.551	
Adjusted R^2	.124	
N of cases (unweighted)	554	

TABLE 2 *Continued*

	Blacks	
	b	beta
Demographics		
Black	—	—
Hispanic	—	—
Education	.052	.053
	(.043)	
Income	.016	.045
	(.015)	
Gender (1 = male)	−.169	−.058
	(.128)	
Age	−.004	−.046
	(.004)	
Residence (1 = city)	.172	.055
	(.137)	
Region (1 = south)	.068	.023
	(.125)	
Neighborhood		
Safety (day)	−.013	−.006
	(.130)	
Safety (night)	.144	.083
	(.106)	
Neighborhood crime	.120	.071
	(.079)	
Policing		
Media exposure	.311 ★★★	.172
	(.078)	
Personal experience (1 = yes)	.749 ★★★ (d)	.258
	(.139)	
Vicarious experience (1 = yes)	.395 ★★	.134
	(.138)	
Constant		2.510
Adjusted R^2		.191
N of cases (unweighted)		458

	Hispanics	
	b	beta
Demographics		
Black	—	—
Hispanic	—	—
Education	.005	.004
	(.046)	
Income	.007	.015
	(.019)	

Continued

TABLE 2 *Continued*

	Hispanics	
	b	**beta**
Gender (1 = male)	.001	.001
	(.144)	
Age	−.009	−.069
	(.005)	
Residence (1 = city)	.485 ★★	.112
	(.170)	
Region (1 = south)	.226	.056
	(.158)	
Neighborhood		
Safety (day)	−.200	−.085
	(.143)	
Safety (night)	−.076	−.039
	(.121)	
Neighborhood crime	.477 ★★★	.227
	(.095)	
Policing		
Media exposure	.392 ★★★	.175
	(.090)	
Personal experience (1 = yes)	1.200 ★★★ (c,d)	.314
	(.171)	
Vicarious experience (1 = yes)	.503 ★★	.126
	(.170)	
Constant	1.497	
Adjusted R^2	.284	
N of cases (unweighted)	514	

(a) Standard errors are in parentheses.
(b) The white and black slope coefficients are significantly different, p < .05
(c) The white and Hispanic slope coefficients are significantly different, p < .05
(d) The black and Hispanic slope coefficients are significantly different, p < .05
★ p < .05 ★★ p < .01 ★★★ p < .001

and for each racial group separately. The total sample coefficients in Table 2 show that race differences in views of police bias persist net of the influence of the other predictors, supporting hypothesis 1b. In all four models—bias against individuals, bias against neighborhoods, police prejudice, and racial profiling—blacks and Hispanics are significantly more likely than whites to adopt a critical view of the police, and—consistent with the racial hierarchy thesis—Hispanics' assessments of police bias are intermediate between the views of whites, who are less negative, and those of blacks, who are more negative. (8)

Several of the coefficients associated with the remaining predictors in the total sample columns of Table 2 are significant in at least three of the four models: younger people, persons exposed to media reports on police misconduct, and those who have personally experienced police bias are more likely to perceive all four types of bias. In addition, increasing education, city residence, and living in a neighborhood with a serious crime problem each significantly increases perceptions of bias in three of the four models.

The group-specific coefficients in Table 2 allow for an examination of racial differences in the effects of the predictors on attitudes toward racialized policing. Model 1 presents results for bias against minority individuals. The demographic variables have generally limited and inconsistent effects on citizen perceptions of this type of police bias, although social class does have some effect. Among whites, higher education increases perceptions of bias against individuals; among blacks, higher income increases these perceptions; but neither education nor income shapes Hispanics' attitudes in this area. Similarly, the three dimensions of neighborhood crime have limited effects, though the feeling that crime is serious in one's neighborhood increases blacks' and Hispanics' perceptions of police bias, and fears about safety (during the day) does so for blacks.

As predicted by hypothesis 2a, exposure to media accounts of police misconduct significantly increases perceptions of police bias against minority individuals among all three racial groups—though difference-in-slopes tests indicate that the effect of media exposure is not significantly stronger among blacks and Hispanics than among whites, as hypothesis 2b predicted. Hypothesis 3a predicted that personal and vicarious experience with police bias would amplify the perception that police discriminate against minority individuals, and hypothesis 3b predicted that this effect would be strongest among blacks and Hispanics. We found that personal (but not vicarious) experience with police discrimination significantly shapes perceived bias among blacks and Hispanics (but not among whites), and, consistent with hypothesis 3b, these effects are significantly stronger among blacks and Hispanics than among whites. Moreover, as indicated by the magnitudes of the standardized coefficients associated with the media and personal experience variables, these effects are among the strongest in the model.

Model 2 in Table 2 reports the effects of the predictors on perceived bias against minority neighborhoods. In this model, higher education among whites, and higher education and income among blacks, increase perceptions of police bias; age is significant for whites and blacks, with older members of both groups reporting less perceived bias; and the remaining demographic predictors are largely unimportant. The view that neighborhood crime is high increases whites' perceptions of police bias against minority neighborhoods; and fears about safety (at night) increase blacks' perceptions of bias; safety fears (during the day), on the other hand, decrease blacks' and Hispanics' perceptions of bias. For each racial group, exposure to media reports of police misconduct significantly influences perceptions of differential police treatment of neighborhoods, strongly supporting hypothesis 2a. Contrary to the prediction of hypothesis 2b, however, we found no white-black or white-Hispanic differences in the effects of media exposure, though we did find that the effect of the media variable is significantly stronger for blacks than for Hispanics. Similarly, personal (but not vicarious) experience with police discrimination increases blacks' and Hispanics' perceptions of bias, lending partial support to hypothesis 3a. The differences with whites are not significant, despite hypothesis 2b's predictions.

The third model in Table 2 summarizes findings for perceptions of police prejudice. Consistent with earlier results, the demographic and neighborhood crime factors have only sporadic effects on perceptions of prejudice, though black and Hispanic city dwellers have higher levels than their suburban counterparts; and neighborhood crime increases perceptions of prejudice among blacks and Hispanics. Media exposure and both personal and vicarious experience with police misconduct, on the other hand, increase perceptions among all three racial groups that police officers are racially prejudiced, again providing strong support for hypotheses 2a and 3a. As before, however, the largely uniform effects of these variables across racial groups are not consistent with hypotheses 2b and 3b.

Model 4 in Table 2 reports results for the racial profiling index. Again, demographic (9) and other control factors play only a small role in accounting for citizens' perceptions and evaluations of racial profiling. As predicted, however, media exposure strongly shapes perceptions; and either personal or vicarious experience with police bias significantly increases perceptions that racial profiling is widespread and unacceptable. Again, evidence of significant minority-white differences of the kind predicted by hypotheses 2b and 3b is weak.

In sum, the demographic factors (other than race) tend to have only sporadic effects in each model; this finding is consistent with the literature on public perceptions of racial discrimination in other institutional arenas (housing, jobs, education) documenting limited or weak demographic effects (Kluegel and Bobo 2001; Sigelman and Welch 1991). Supporting hypothesis 2a, we found that exposure to media accounts of police misconduct is significant in all models for each group. Hypothesis 2b's prediction of stronger media effects among minority than among white citizens was not supported, however. Hypothesis 3a predicted that personal or vicarious experience with police bias would increase citizens' overall perceptions of racialized policing among all groups. The personal experience variant of hypothesis 3a receives strong support; evidence for the vicarious experience version of the hypothesis is somewhat weaker, with significant effects present in the prejudice and profiling, but not in the individual- or neighborhood-bias, models. Hypothesis 3b also received partial support. Compared to whites, personal experience with police bias significantly increases perceptions of biased policing for blacks and Hispanics in model 1, and for Hispanics in model 4. Vicarious experience with police bias, though not as consistent a predictor as personal experience, is nevertheless significant in two of the four models for each racial group, lending partial support to hypothesis 3a—though the racial differences predicted by hypothesis 3b are not present. The fact that there are few racial differences with regard to the effect of personal and vicarious experience on perceptions of police bias is consistent with some other studies that have found that the effect of certain kinds of personal experience—such as racial profiling—is so powerful that it colors attitudes toward the police irrespective of race (Weitzer and Tuch 2002).

CONCLUSION

Race structures citizen views of police racial bias, as it does other aspects of policing. In all four models, blacks and Hispanics are more likely than whites to believe that police bias is a problem. Blacks, however, are more likely to perceive such bias than Hispanics, net of other factors. This finding helps address one unanswered question in the literature on police-minority relations—whether blacks and Hispanics share a minority-group perspective or whether perceptions take the form of a white-Hispanic-black racial hierarchy. On the issue of racialized policing, we find that, consistent with the racial-hierarchy pattern, blacks and Hispanics do differ significantly. Indeed, on some questions, Hispanics are much less likely to perceive bias than are blacks. For instance, blacks are more likely to perceive police discrimination against Hispanics than Hispanics themselves are to hold this belief, and blacks are more likely than Hispanics to say that Hispanic neighborhoods are discriminated against (vs. white neighborhoods) and to believe that Hispanic drivers are racially profiled (compared to white drivers). Blacks are thus more inclined to perceive racial bias against both minority groups. These findings indicate that "minority" perceptions are not monolithic: in terms of racially biased policing, Hispanics differ in some important ways from African Americans. One reason that the two groups differ, at least with regard to their personal experiences, may have to do with their visibility. For instance, blacks may be more vulnerable than Hispanics to traffic stops by police because their skin color heightens their visibility. But further research is needed to account more fully for black-Hispanic differences in relations with police. It may be that black and Hispanic views are issue-specific: on some issues most Hispanics and blacks may agree, while on other issues there may be less consensus (see Weitzer and Tuch 2004a, 2004b).

Americans are overwhelmingly opposed in principle to racially biased law enforcement. When asked in one poll whether it is the responsibility of the federal government to ensure that minorities and whites receive equal treatment from the police and the courts, large majorities of whites, Hispanics, and African Americans answered affirmatively (Washington Post 1995). But support for the principle of equal justice does not necessarily mean that one believes the system dispenses unequal justice. Our data indicate that many whites believe that the system operates impartially. Over three-quarters of whites think that police treat individual blacks and Hispanics the same as whites; a substantial majority of whites take the same view of minority and white neighborhoods; among whites who believe that police officers are prejudiced, most take the position that prejudice is mild, "somewhat common" instead of "very common"; and only one-third of whites believe that police engage in racial profiling of minority drivers—stopping them more frequently than whites for the same kinds of traffic violations. (10) That many whites are skeptical with regard to police discrimination, or see it as isolated and episodic rather than widespread, is consistent with their views of racial discrimination elsewhere in American society (Hochschild 1995; Schuman et al. 1997). In one poll, for instance, only 17% of whites—compared to 44% of blacks—thought that blacks are discriminated against "a lot" in America (Washington Post, 12 June 1997). For most whites, racial discrimination in general, and police discrimination in particular, is not a serious problem in America. Minorities, by contrast, tend to perceive racial discrimination in a wide range of institutional arenas, including housing, employment, and education (Hochschild 1995; Schuman et al. 1997).

Blacks and Hispanics are also significantly more likely than whites to report that they have personally been discriminated against by the police and that this has happened to another member of their household. While Hispanics are less likely than blacks to report these kinds of experiences, the percentage of Hispanics who do so is closer to that of blacks than it is to that of whites—departing somewhat from the racial hierarchy pattern.

Of course, perceived experience with police bias is not necessarily equivalent to actual discrimination—since the sheer exercise of police authority (typically in a brusque and authoritarian manner) may be construed as racial bias by citizens (Sykes and Clark 1975; Wilson 1972). But, as is true for racial discrimination in other spheres, there is at least a rough aggregate correspondence between actual practice and blacks' and Hispanics' reported experiences of police treatment. Our respondents' self-reports are consistent with evidence from street observations of police-citizen interactions and records of police stops, which indicate that police indeed tend to view minorities with a high degree of suspicion and as having criminal propensities. Minorities tend to be stopped more often than whites (Fagan and Davies 2000; Harris 2002) and to be treated more harshly in encounters (Hepburn 1978; Smith 1986; Terrill and Reisig 2003). Similarly, the high percentage of blacks and Hispanics who believe that police prejudice is widespread in the nation is consistent with data on police officers themselves. As Jefferson concludes, "All the major British and North American studies, from the early post-war period on, agree that negative, stereotypical, prejudiced, and hostile attitudes to blacks are rife amongst police officers (1988:522)."

To explore further these racial differences, we examined several possible predictors of perceptions. Most studies of police-citizen relations focus on demographic variables, which, we find, do not fully exhaust the range of determinants of public opinion. Citizen views are also strongly influenced by certain nondemographic factors.

First, personal and vicarious experience of racially biased policing shapes perceptions of police bias, net of other factors. For blacks and Hispanics, such personal experience significantly increases perceptions of racialized policing in all four models. This perception is not the case for whites (with one exception). Vicarious experience significantly affects perceived police bias in two of the four models for each racial group. A similar pattern is found with respect to discrimination in other arenas, such as jobs and housing. One study, for instance, found that blacks, Hispanics, and Asians who felt that they had personally experienced job discrimination were more likely to perceive job discrimination against their minority group generally (Kluegel and Bobo 2001).

A second key finding is the mass media's role in shaping perceptions of racialized policing. Repeated exposure to media reports on police abuse (i.e., excessive force, verbal abuse, corruption) is a strong predictor of the belief that police bias exists, is widespread, and is unacceptable. Media effects are extremely robust—operating for all three racial groups in all four models, net of other factors. People who frequently hear or read about incidents of police misconduct, as transmitted by the media, are inclined to conclude that the police engage in racial profiling, are prejudiced, and discriminate against minority individuals and neighborhoods. Though it is usually overlooked by researchers who study public perceptions of the police, the mass media appears to be an important determinant of those perceptions.

As indicated earlier, much of the literature documents race differences but does not adequately explain them. Our extension of the group-position thesis holds that views of social institutions will be influenced by group interests and perceived threats. Dominant groups should perceive the police as an institution allied with their interests, whereas minorities should be more inclined to view the police as contributing to their subordination. These predictions are generally supported by our findings. Whites tend to minimize or discount the existence of racialized policing and perhaps view charges of police racism as a threat to a revered institution. Blacks are inclined to believe that police bias is common, and many Hispanics share this view. Both groups are interested in curbing abuses of citizens, particularly minority citizens, who are disproportionately the recipients of mistreatment. Greater controls on the police may have the effect of advancing the group interests of blacks and Hispanics (Weitzer and Tuch 2004b).

Our findings highlight the role of both micro- and macro-level factors in fostering racial differences in evaluations of the police: The greater tendency for blacks and Hispanics to perceive bias is largely a function of their disproportionate adverse experiences with officers and exposure to media reports of police abuse. Views of the police are thus related to racial differences not only in general group-position relationships but also in real or perceived group vulnerability to abusive practices, which is reinforced by both personal experience and exposure to media reports of abuse.

⋆ *Research for this article was funded by the National Institute of Justice, Office of Justice Programs, U.S. Department of Justice, Grant 2001-IJ-CX-0016. We are also grateful for the support of the Columbian Research Fellows program at George Washington University. Direct correspondence to Ronald Weitzer, Department of Sociology, George Washington University, Washington, DC 20052. E-mail: weitzer@gwu.edu.*

NOTES

1.   In the present survey, Hispanics and blacks overwhelmingly supported an increase, in their city, in the number of officers patrolling the streets in police cars (80% for both groups) and on foot patrol (69% and 80%, respectively) as well as "more police surveillance of areas where street crimes occur frequently" (85% and 88%, respectively). White support for these changes was similarly high.

2.   The American Association for Public Opinion Research response rate definitions can be viewed at www.aapor.org.

3.   A detailed demographic panel analysis is available at www.knowledgenetworks.com.

4.   We recognize that only one type of vicarious experience is measured by our question. It does not include other associates, such as friends, coworkers, and neighbors.

5.   Because our media-exposure measure is based on respondents' self-reports, some caution is in order in interpreting media effects. Some self-selection may be involved in exposure to media coverage of the police, with acutely interested persons being more attentive than others. Our media variable is also fairly broad, asking about exposure to reports of police abuse anywhere in the country, which may or may not include the respondent's city of residence. An alternative measure would ask specifically about media coverage of incidents in the respondent's city.

6.   We use the term "racial bias" as a construct referring to the four types of outcomes described in this paragraph, while recognizing that two of the questions refer to disparate treatment of individuals and neighborhoods, which may or may not reflect outright racial discrimination.

7.   All the cross-tabulated relationships discussed in this section are statistically significant (p < .001).

8.   Hispanics were asked to identify their ancestry as Mexican, Puerto Rican, Cuban, Central or South American, Caribbean, or other Hispanic. No significant subgroup differences on perceived police bias were found. Because of the small sample sizes for some of these subgroups, this finding should be considered tentative. It is also for this reason that our primary analyses compare the three major racial groups rather than the Hispanic nationality groups.

9.   A previous study (Weitzer and Tuch 2002) reported class effects on attitudes toward racial profiling among African Americans, with more educated blacks expressing more disapproval of the practice and greater awareness of its existence than less educated blacks. We suspected that the absence of class effects among blacks (in model 4, Table 2) was attributable to differences in the measures of profiling used in the two studies. To test this, we selected from our four-item index of profiling attitudes the two questions that we replicated from our earlier study—approval of profiling and assessments of whether the practice is widespread—and fit logistic regression models to the data for blacks. We found class effects consistent with our earlier findings: Higher-income blacks are more likely than lower-income blacks to disapprove of profiling, and more educated blacks are more likely than their less educated counterparts to believe that profiling is widespread.

10. The only exception to this pattern is that a majority of whites believe that racial profiling is widespread in the U.S. (but not in their city or neighborhood). Curiously, in an apparent contradiction, whites are twice as likely to believe that profiling is widespread than to believe that blacks or Hispanics are stopped more frequently than whites.

Ronald Weitzer, George Washington University

Steven A. Tuch, George Washington University

REFERENCES

Baker, Lawrence, M. Kate Bundorf, Sara Singer, and Todd Wagner. 2003. Validity of the Survey of Health and Internet and Knowledge Network's Panel and Sampling. Unpublished paper, Stanford University.

Bayley, David, and Harold Mendelsohn. 1969. Minorities and the Police. Free Press.

Berrens, Robert. 2003. "The Advent of Internet Surveys for Political Research: A Comparison of Telephone and Internet Samples." Political Analysis 11:1–22.

Blumer, Herbert. 1958. "Race Prejudice as a Sense of Group Position." Pacific Sociological Review 1:3–7.

Bobo, Lawrence. 1999. "Prejudice as Group Position." Journal of Social Issues 55:445–72.

Bobo, Lawrence, and Vincent Hutchings. 1996. "Perceptions of Racial Group Competition." American Sociological Review 61:951–72.

Brown, Ben, and William Benedict. 2002. "Perceptions of the Police." Policing 25:543–80.

Cohn, Steven, and Steven Barkan. 2004. "Racial Prejudice and Public Attitudes about the Punishment of Criminals." Pp. 33–47 in For the Common Good, edited by R. Miller and S. Browning. Carolina Academic Press.

Dennis, J. Michael, and Rick Li. 2003. "Effects of Panel Attrition on Survey Estimates." Paper presented at the annual meeting of the American Association for Public Opinion Research, Nashville, TN, May.

Fagan, Jeffrey and Garth Davies. 2000. "Street Stops and Broken Windows: Terry, Race, and Disorder in New York City." Fordham Urban Law Journal 28:457–504.

Gallagher, Catherine, Edward Maguire, Stephen Mastrofski, and Michael Reisig. 2001. The Public Image of the Police. International Association of Chiefs of Police.

Harris, David. 2002. Profiles in Injustice. New Press.

Hepburn, John. 1978. "Race and the Decision to Arrest." Journal of Research in Crime and Delinquency 15:54–73.

Hochschild, Jennifer. 1995. Facing Up to the American Dream. Princeton University Press.

Hurwitz, Jon, and Mark Peffley. 1997. "Public Perceptions of Race and Crime: The Role of Racial Stereotypes." American Journal of Political Science 41:375–401.

Jackson, Pamela Irving. 1989. Minority Group Threat, Crime, and Policing. Praeger.

Jefferson, Tony. 1988. "Race, Crime, and Policing." International Journal of the Sociology of Law 16:521–39.

Kaminski, Robert and Eric Jefferis. 1998. "The Effect of a Violent Televised Arrest on Public Perceptions of the Police." Policing 21:683–706.

Kinder, Donald R., and Lynn M. Sanders. 1996. Divided by Color: Racial Politics and Democratic Ideals. University of Chicago Press.

Kluegel, James, and Lawrence Bobo. 2001. "Perceived Group Discrimination and Policy Attitudes." Pp. 163–213 in Urban Inequality: Evidence from Four Cities, edited by A. O'Connor, C. Tilly, and L. Bobo. Russell Sage Foundation.

Krosnick, Jon, and Lin Chait Chang. 2001. "A Comparison of Random Digit Dialing Telephone Survey Methodology with Internet Survey Methodology as Implemented by Knowledge Networks and Harris Interactive." Paper presented at the annual conference of the American Association for Public Opinion Research, Montreal, Canada, May.

Schuman, Howard, Charlotte Steeh, Lawrence Bobo, and Maria Krysan. 1997. Racial Attitudes in America. Harvard University Press.

Sigelman, Lee, and Susan Welch. 1991 Black Americans' Views of Racial Inequality. Cambridge University Press.

Sigelman, Lee, Susan Welch, Timothy Bledsoe, and Michael Combs. 1997. "Police Brutality and Public Perceptions of Racial Discrimination." Political Research Quarterly 50:777–91.

Smith, Douglas. 1986. "The Neighborhood Context of Police Behavior." Crime and Justice 8:313–41.

Sykes, Richard, and John Clark. 1975. "A Theory of Deference Exchange in Police-Civilian Encounters." American Journal of Sociology 81:584–600.

Terrill, William, and Michael Reisig. 2003. "Neighborhood Context and Police Use of Force." Journal of Research in Crime and Delinquency 40:291–321.

Tuch, Steven A., and Ronald Weitzer. 1997. "Racial Differences in Attitudes toward the Police." Public Opinion Quarterly 61:642–63.

Tyler, Tom, and Yuen Huo. 2002. Trust in the Law. Russell Sage Foundation.

Washington Post Company. 1995. Washington Post/Harvard School of Public Health/ Kaiser Foundation poll, 20 July–28 September 1995. Lexis-Nexis.

Weitzer, Ronald. 1995. Policing under Fire: Communal Conflict and Police-Community Relations in Northern Ireland. SUNY Press.

———. 2000. "Racialized Policing." Law and Society Review 34:129–55.

———. 2002. "Incidents of Police Misconduct and Public Opinion?" Journal of Criminal Justice 30:397–408.

Weitzer, Ronald, and Steven A. Tuch. 1999. "Race, Class, and Perceptions of Discrimination by the Police." Crime and Delinquency 45:494–507.

———. 2002. "Perceptions of Racial Profiling: Race, Class, and Personal Experience?" Criminology 40:435–56.

———. 2004a. "Race and Perceptions of Police Misconduct." Social Problems 51:305–25.

———. 2004b. "Reforming the Police: Racial Differences in Public Support for Change." Criminology 42:391–416.

Wilson, James Q. 1972. "The Police in the Ghetto." Pp. 51–97 in The Police and the Community, edited by R. Steadman. Johns Hopkins University Press.

3

Policing Space, Policing Race: Social Control Imperatives and Police Discretionary Decisions

Sandra Bass

The tenuous and often contentious relationship between racial minorities and the police is a perennial concern of scholars, policymakers, and the public. Despite the centrality of race in the historical development of the police, as well as in contemporary criminal justice policies and police practices, there are few scholarly attempts to develop a construct for understanding this relationship. This essay discusses the interactive relationship between race, space, and policing in U.S. history. These three factors have been central in forwarding race-based social control and have been intertwined in public policy and police practices since the earliest days of this country's history. Despite the demise of de jure segregation and discrimination, de facto discriminatory policies and practices perpetuate a substantially authoritarian, regulatory, and punitive relationship between racial minorities and the police. Drug-war related, quality of life, and zero tolerance policing are integral to the social control imperative in the contemporary policing of racial minorities. This essay concludes with a discussion of avenues for change that could improve policing in a multicultural democracy.

The interactive relationship between race, space, and policing has been of social and political significance since the earliest days of American history. Monitoring the movement of slaves was a central concern for plantation masters and slave patrollers. The desire to regulate and subjugate the behavior of newly manumitted slaves was the primary impetus for creating new legal rules against vagrancy and loitering in the post-antebellum South. The rise of Jim Crow and the location and construction of urban ghettos and public housing were deliberate efforts to promote social control and isolation through racial containment. For the better part of our history, race has been a central determinant in the definition, construction, and regulation of public spaces. Some authors have even used the analogy of internal colonization to describe the relationship between African-American communities, the state, and the police (see Staples, 2001; Blauner, 1969).

Although the experiences of African Americans and the police are widely known and documented, history shows that the relationship between race, space, and social control also holds for other racial minorities. For example, in the 19th century, Chinese immigrants were harshly and legally discriminated against in California. Forced to live in ethnic enclaves, "Chinatowns" became a central feature on the West Coast. Soon, local municipalities created special Chinatown police squads to police Chinese workers. Divorced from "polite" society, the rule of law seemed to have limited bearing over police activities in various Chinatowns, and blatant police corruption was common (see, e.g., Friedman, 1981). A contemporary example of differential treatment for racially identified spaces is illustrated in one author's contention that the Los Angeles Police Department (LAPD) consciously sacrificed Koreatown during the L.A. uprisings in order to concentrate limited police resources on more affluent Anglo neighborhoods on the periphery (Cho, 1993).

The history of Latinos in the U.S. indicates a similar pattern of separation and social control. Edward Escobar's (1999) excellent history of the relationship between Mexican Americans and the LAPD argues that the emergence of a race-based political consciousness among Mexican Americans in Los Angeles was largely due to egregious police practices in Mexican-American barrios. The "Zoot Suit" riots and the "Sleepy Lagoon Murder Trial" are the best-known examples of discriminatory police actions against Latinos (Mirande, 1987; Escobar, 1999). Indeed, the U.S. Civil Rights Commission held hearings to discuss tensions between Mexican Americans and the police. The following excerpt illustrates the similarity of experience between Mexican Americans and African Americans with respect to policing:

> [The Commission] heard frequent allegations that law enforcement officers discriminated against Mexican-Americans. Such discrimination includes more frequent use of excessive force against Mexican-Americans than against Anglos, discriminatory treatment of juveniles, and harassment and discourteous treatment toward Mexican-Americans in general. Complaints also were heard that police protection in Mexican American neighborhoods was less adequate than other areas. The Commission's investigations showed that belief in law

enforcement prejudice is widespread and indicative of a serious problem of police/community relations between the police and Mexican-Americans in the Southwest (U.S. Civil Rights Commission, 1970).

Urban spaces are socially and politically constructed to meet certain goals, ends, visions, and dreams. Ethnic/racial separation has historically been a central feature, and in some instances, [the] goal in the development of American cities, and federal, state, and local governments as well as private [sectors] have historically engaged in a range of discriminatory practices to create and preserve racial discrimination and segregation. The social construction of space has had a significant impact on the development of policing in America. As Steve Herbert (1997) notes, the police are the domestic institution responsible for preserving domestic spatial sovereignty. Thus, how the police conceptualize territory is critical to understanding police work. In his book, Policing Space: Territoriality and the Los Angeles Police Department, Herbert discusses six "normative orders" in police organizations that instruct how they exercise their territoriality: the law, bureaucratic imperatives, adventure/machismo, safety, competence, and morality. Surprisingly, even though Herbert's rich ethnographic descriptions of police behavior often mention race in passing, he does not discuss the ways in which race affects police attitudes and behavior in the policing of spaces. Some have argued that class, not race, is the more critical determinant driving police behavior. In the classic critical criminological assessment of the police, The Iron Fist and The Velvet Glove, the authors subsume the issue of race under that of class, arguing that police brutality against racial minorities reflects the broader goal of capitalist repression of the working class (Platt et al., 1982).

Hall et al. (1978) place race, space, crime, and social control at the center of their analysis. In their detailed analysis of the emergence of "mugging" as a political issue in London in the 1970s, Hall et al. deftly exposed the ways in which the social and political construction of this "crisis" delineated the institutional imperatives that "reproduce" racial disadvantage. "Racism is not simply the discriminatory attitudes of the personnel with whom blacks come into contact. It is the specific mechanism which 'reproduces' the black labour force, from one generation to another, in the places and positions which are race specific" (Ibid.). This perspective recognizes the connection between class, race, and social control, yet clearly identifies the structural conditions that perpetuate racialized spaces and experiences.

Although the connection between race, space, and policing is useful for understanding tensions between the police and many racial minorities, this analysis will focus primarily on the experiences of African Americans. The dearth of research on police/community relations with other racial minorities is one reason for the more limited discussion. However, the enforced racial segregation that African Americans experienced is particularly unique and insightful. As Massey and Denton (1993) note, "no group in the history of the United States has ever experienced the sustained high levels of residential segregation imposed on blacks." The linkages between race, space, and policing become clear in reviewing the history of legally sanctioned racial discrimination and residential segregation of African Americans and the development of policing. Government-supported racial discrimination and segregation have deeply affected the organizing ethos and practices of U.S. policing. A legacy of biased police discretionary decision-making persists beyond the demise of de jure racial discrimination, perpetuating a relationship between the police and racial minorities that is primarily authoritarian, regulatory, and punitive in character. Further, contemporary policy decisions at the federal, state, and local levels continue to perpetuate a contentious relationship between the police and racial minorities based on social control rather than public service imperatives.

POLICING SPACE, POLICING RACE: THE AFRICAN-AMERICAN EXPERIENCE

The American journey through slavery left an indelible mark on social and political institutions, particularly the police. Although informal policing mechanisms began in the colonial period, the emergence of a semi-formal, organized policing force can be traced to slavery (Williams and Murphy, 1990; Reichel, 1999). Under the slave regime, controlling a slave labor population that in some instances equaled or surpassed the size of the master class was a pressing social control problem. The threat of slave insurrection and the recurrent problem of slaves fleeing captivity necessitated the creation of a means of regulating the movement of slaves. Slaves moving beyond the boundaries of plantations were required to have passage papers that authorized them to do so. In the late 18th century, loosely organized slave patrols were created to patrol and enforce these regulations, and to engage in what Franklin and Schweninger (1999) have referred to as "the hunt." South Carolina, a state in which slaves outnumbered whites, was the first state to institute such a patrol.

Slave patrols were initially comprised of volunteers. Over time, particularly with the passage of the Fugitive Slave Act in 1850, state governments were given broad authority to compel individuals to join slave patrols. Slave patrols were vested with virtually unlimited coercive authority in their charge to monitor the movement of slaves and track down runaways. In many instances, slave patrols could and did enter slave homes with impunity. Slave patrollers, or "paterollers" as slaves came to call them, had the authority to physically punish runaway slaves. Patrollers were widely feared by slaves, since whippings and other extremely violent actions were not uncommon (Williams and Murphy, 1990; Reichel, 1999). A former slave recounts how one persistent runaway submitted to self-immolation rather than face the wrath of patrollers.

> There was once a runaway slave who had been chased at different times for four years. At last a set of patrollers came in with their dogs and said they were determined to catch him. They ran him for two days. Once in a while he would mislead the dogs and make them double on their tracks and he would

gain a little rest. Eventually they would again pick up the trail and you could hear the hounds as they ran; say, here he goes sing-a-ding; there he goes, sing-a-ding. At last, finding that he could not escape, he ran deliberately into a blazing furnace and was burned to death rather than be caught and suffer the tortures that awaited him (WPA Slave Narratives Project).

With the end of slavery, Southern whites were faced with new economic and social control dilemmas. On the one hand, the slave-owning class was dependent on black labor to sustain the largely agricultural economy. On the other hand, ensuring the social and political subordination of newly manumitted slaves was essential if the ideology of white supremacy were to continue to reign. An important legal tool for pursuing these aims was the passage of broadly defined vagrancy and loitering statutes that came to be known as the Black Codes. Mississippi and South Carolina became the first states to pass such legislation near the end of 1865. Even though many of these laws were racially neutral, the intention was clearly to control the black population. By law, blacks were required each January to exhibit to the government evidence of employment for the coming year. African Americans were also prohibited from engaging in a broad range of other "disorderly offenses," such as using insulting gestures or language, engaging in malicious mischief, preaching the Gospel without a license, or taking on employment other than as farmers or servants without paying an annual tax (Williams and Murphy, 1990). Those who violated the codes received punishments ranging from fines to serving on chain gangs or doing involuntary labor on a plantation. The Black Codes essentially created a set of legal tools for ensuring the continued subordination of black labor to white economic power.

As the Black Codes came under legal attack, Southern states aggressively pursued radical racial segregation to ensure white supremacy and black subordination. One of the great ironies of history is that a practice that became synonymous with the South actually began in the North. In his classic pre-Civil War treatise on American social and political life, Democracy in America, Alexis de Toqueville (2000/1835) was surprised to find, "the prejudice of race appears to be stronger in the states that have abolished slavery than in those were it still exists and nowhere is it so intolerant as in those states where servitude has never been known." By 1860, the system of segregation permeated all aspects of black life in the free states (Woodward, 1968).

In the South, the proliferation of Jim Crow grew out of economic crisis, political opportunism, and racial fears. With the demise of congressional reconstruction in 1877, white southerners were left to deal with the "race problem" on their own terms. In the 1890s, Southern states experienced an economic depression that some estimated to be greater in magnitude than the Great Depression (Ibid.). White solidarity was viewed as essential for the continued economic dominance of the white population. Ensuring that blacks did not vote was key to retaining white power. Political disenfranchisement of the black population flourished through devices such as grandfather clauses, white-only primaries, literacy and civic exams, and intimidation and violence aimed at deterring black voters from going to the polls. Further, as Southern states began to urbanize, fears of "race-mixing" began to mount.

Within this context, Jim Crow advanced rapidly as a means of resolving multiple problems. Unlike the North, residential racial segregation was not aggressively pursued in the early years of Jim Crow. As Massey and Denton (1993: 26) note, Jim Crow in the South did not initially increase segregation or reduce black-white contact, but rather regulated the nature of interracial social contact. The intent of Jim Crow was to continually reaffirm and remind the black population of their lesser status or "place" in the larger society. Southern localities passed amazingly elaborate regulations to govern black life in shared public spaces and interactions between the races. Some of the regulations are astounding for their attention to detail. For example, some codes regulated the height, size, and color of Jim Crow signs (Woodward, 1968). However, legal rules do not fully represent the extent of Jim Crowism in the South. Practices often anticipated and sometimes exceeded the law. Since almost every aspect of black public life was regulated, and every white regardless of formal capacity or social station was viewed as superior to blacks, every white person was expected to participate in policing the racial lines (Woodward, 1968; Myrdal, 1944).

The Jim Crow laws put the authority of the state or city in the voice of the street car conductor, the railway brakeman, the bus driver, the theater usher, and also into the voice of the hoodlum of the public parks and playgrounds (Woodward, 1968).

Essentially, African Americans lived in a police state in which every aspect of shared public life was proscribed. Formal police organizations under this system were responsible for upholding the formal and informal social order. The formal police in the segregated South represented the South's repressive civil order and the ideology of white supremacy overall. "He stands not only for civic order as defined by formal laws and regulations, but also for white supremacy and a whole set of social customs associated with the concept" (Myrdal, 1944: 535). Police brutality was frequently employed to punish insubordination and suspected criminals, and was another means of "keeping the Negro in his place more generally" (ibid.: 540). Moreover, the police often overlooked or participated in overt acts of violence against blacks who offended against the reigning order.

Black migration from the South to the North surged after World Wars I and II. Northern industrial cities such as New York, Detroit, and Chicago were primary sites for black migration. As the black population grew, so did the tools and means for containing newly arrived blacks in burgeoning ghettos. Race riots broke out with some regularity in Northern cities between 1900 and 1920, largely due to black migration (Sugrue, 1996: 29). Federal policies played a significant role in encouraging white flight to the suburbs and restricting African Americans to specific inner-city neighborhoods. (1) Local political leaders, real estate agents and developers, and community-based neighborhood preservationists used various tactics to discourage blacks from moving to white neighborhoods. In the postwar city, "blackness and whiteness assumed a spatial definition" (Ibid.: 9).

Blacks with the temerity to buy homes in "white" neighborhoods were often met with violence and intimidation. In Chicago, 58 Black homes were bombed between 1917 and 1921. One black real estate agent had his Chicago home and office bombed seven times in one year (Massey and Denton, 1993). Over 200 incidents of white antagonism directed at blacks moving into formerly white neighborhoods were recorded in the years between World War II and the 1960s in Detroit. Actions included "harassment, mass demonstrations, picketing, effigy burning, window breaking, arson, vandalism, and physical attacks" (Sugrue, 1996: 233).

These incidents were often community-organized events. White women—homemakers—were often leaders in acts of neighborhood resistance. The high participation rates of women offered a measure of protection against police actions since the police were often reluctant to arrest women and children (Ibid.). Even when gender participation was more balanced, the police were often slow to respond to acts of white violence against blacks and in some instances allowed whites to engage in terrorist attacks against black homeowners. (2)

Although less widely recognized, racial discrimination and social control through residential racial segregation were also factors in the development of Western cities with appreciable black populations. In Los Angeles, for example, the city passed a law known as the Shenk rule that permitted saloons to charge blacks more than whites for beer (Bunch, 1990: 105). Racial segregation was also a primary tool of social control and discrimination. In early Los Angeles, residential racial mixing was more common than racial segregation, and African Americans enjoyed one of the highest home-owning rates in the country. (3) Beginning in the mid-1910s, spatial social control and residential segregation were aggressively pursued through a variety of means. Fear of the establishment of a black political power base in Watts led to its annexation in the 1920s (Ibid.: 111). As the black population increased in the years after World War I and World War II, white homeowners used new tactics to deter blacks from moving into their neighborhoods. The most common tool was the residential racial covenant, which prevented the sale of real estate to blacks for a proscribed period of time. Racial covenants, along with other formal and informal acts, pushed blacks into the overcrowded neighborhoods of Watts and South Central L.A.

Developments in Northern and Western cities were directed toward spatially defining racial subordination. The inability to live beyond the boundaries of the ghettos and to move freely within the city without fear of police harassment severely restricted the civil liberties of African Americans. In 1963, one black minister in Detroit argued that the system of racial segregation in which those with "the desire and ability to move without the right to move" amounted to "refined slavery" (quoted in Sugrue, 1996).

This brief historical review of the connection between racial subordination and spatial development in the U.S. is relevant to understanding contemporary police practices for several reasons. Legalized discrimination has had a profound impact on the police. As the primary agents of domestic law enforcement, the police were responsible for upholding and enforcing discriminatory laws. Further, the record shows that racial minorities have historically been viewed as objects of law enforcement and social control rather than as citizens entitled to civil protections. The centrality of race in the formation and organizing ethos of the police is often ignored, yet it is critical for understanding the development of policing as an institution.

Second, federal, state, and local governments played an active role in creating and preserving race-based spatial residential patterns. History shows that blatantly discriminatory and facially neutral polices that were discriminatory in practice were implemented primarily to segregate and discriminate against African Americans. The effects of these decisions are evident today in the persistent patterns of racial segregation that are readily visible in most major American cities. Further, policy decisions, particularly those concerning criminal justice at all levels of government, remain a central factor in perpetuating the differential treatment and outcomes of minorities who come in contact with the police.

Third, spatial segregation provided a means for differential delivery and distribution of public goods and services to black communities. As Gunnar Myrdal (1944) noted, residential segregation created "an artificial city…that permits any prejudice on the part of public officials to be freely vented on Negroes without hurting whites." In other words, residential segregation provides a means by which wholly different standards of public service could be delivered without adversely affecting the white community. As the police are essentially a spatially deployed public service, the interaction between race and space are central to understanding police practices. Policing in the segregated zones has historically been qualitatively different from that in predominately white neighborhoods. Further, residential segregation created cognitive boundaries that defined those "places" that were relegated to racial minorities and those that were not. African Americans and other racial minorities who ventured outside their neighborhoods were often subject to police harassment for having the temerity to circulate "out of their place."

Perhaps Williams and Murphy (1990: 28) put it most succinctly when they so famously noted:

> The fact that the legal order not only countenanced but sustained slavery, segregation, and discrimination for most of our nation's history and the fact that the police were bound to uphold that order—set a pattern for police behavior and attitudes toward minority communities that has persisted until the present day. That pattern includes the idea that minorities have fewer civil rights, that the task of the police is to keep them under control, and that the police have little responsibility for protecting them from crime within their communities.

Finally, despite the demise of de jure racial discrimination, police policies and practices perpetuate a relationship between the police and racial minorities that is substantially authoritarian and regulatory in character. In the contemporary setting, this relationship is most pronounced in the police policies and practices developed to contend with the war on drugs, to address urban disorder, and the growth of gang membership.

THE WAR ON DRUGS—THE NEW JIM CROW? (4)

Police policies and practices associated with the "war on drugs" have been the most influential in perpetuating racially discriminatory police discretionary behavior. With the introduction of crack cocaine and the resulting violence associated with the drug trade, various criminal justice policies and practices have evolved to contend with the "drug problem."

Particularly in the early years of the drug war, intrusive police practices characterized the response of local law enforcement to drugs. Commonly employed strategies have been buy/bust and reverse sting operations, in which police pose as buyers or sellers and then arrest offenders. The serving of "no-knock warrants" to "high-risk" drug offenders, as well aggressive raids on crack houses, were also part of drug war policing (Chambliss, 1994). The LAPD introduced military tactics into the fight against drugs. It pioneered the use of the "battering ram"—a vehicle equipped with a ramming device—to forcibly enter suspected crack houses. At times, police operations in the drug war have been reckless, if not blatantly illegal. For example, in August 1988, 80 police officers from various divisions executed a drug raid on four apartments on Dalton Avenue in South Central Los Angeles. Although officers seized only small amounts of cocaine and marijuana during the raid, the action resulted in "127 separate acts of police vandalism, ranging from doors, walls, and cabinets smashed apart, to smashed piggy banks." One officer was reported to have "swung an ax so wildly as he tore from room to room in the apartments...that his fellow LAPD officers believed he was going to hurt himself or the other policemen in his path" (U.S. Commission on Civil Rights, 1999: 19). Thirty-three people were taken into custody, but only one was charged with possession of drugs. Chief Gates' response to charges of officer misbehavior was customarily tepid: "the officers were trying hard to do the right thing—to solve the gang problem, to solve narcotics trafficking problem. Unfortunately, while doing the right thing, they were doing it in the wrong way" (Schiesl, 1990: 189). Although the police argue that no-knock warrants are necessary for police safety, they are an extremely intrusive practice that have accentuated the perception that inner-city neighborhoods are under military siege.

In recent years, the police practice of racial profiling has emerged as one of the most controversial drug war strategies. Racial profiling initially referred to the police practice of conducting traffic stops for petty offenses under the pretext that individuals stopped are likely involved in more serious criminal activity. Although racial profiling has become the term-of-art to describe a range of race-based discretionary decisions, the practice is most commonly associated with drug profiling. The U.S. Drug Enforcement Agency is credited with introducing race as a variable in drug courier profiles (Glasser, 2000). Drug profiles claim to establish specific criteria for identifying drug couriers. However, the profiles are typically so vague and over-inclusive that virtually anyone can be considered a drug trafficker if the police deem them to be. (See, for example, Cole, 1999; Russell, 1998.)

It is often difficult to document these types of discretionary decisions. However, research conducted in New Jersey and Maryland confirms that some members of these agencies actively used race as a proxy for criminality. In New Jersey, Lamberth (in Harris, 1999) found that even though observational data determined that only 13.2% of drivers on the New Jersey turnpike were black, and that blacks and whites violated the traffic code at roughly the same rates, 73.2% of arrests were of African Americans. In Maryland, a similar phenomenon was found: 72% of those stopped were black, yet only 17.5% of the drivers were black. Further, African Americans were far more likely to be subjected to consent searches than were white drivers. Befitting scientific evaluation, Lamberth subjected both studies to rigorous statistical testing and found the statistical significance for both of these studies was literally "off the charts" (Harris, 1999).

A great deal of racial profiling occurs on what law enforcement agencies deem to be drug courier routes, such as major interstate highways. However, racial profiling is practiced in a broader range of local settings as well. Many African Americans particularly fear being stopped and harassed by police when they venture beyond the borders of the black community. For example, one man discusses his experiences with arbitrary police stops:

> I come from a lower-middle-class black neighborhood, OK, that borders a white neighborhood. One neighborhood is all black, and one is all white. OK, just because we were so close to that neighborhood, we were stopped endlessly and it happened even more when we went up into the suburban community. When we would ride up and out to the suburbs, we were stopped every time we did it (Anderson, 1990: 197).

The experiences of prominent African Americans such as Wesley Snipes, Blair Underwood, and Johnnie Cochran, who have been stopped and questioned as they drove through high-income, white communities confirm that race is a central factor in how the police determine who belongs where. As David Harris writes,

> Driving while black serves as a spatial restriction on African Americans, circumscribing their movements. Put simply, blacks know that police and white residents feel that there are areas in which blacks "do not belong." Often, these are all-white suburban communities or upscale commercial areas. When blacks drive through these areas, they maybe watched and stopped because they are "out of place" (Harris, 1999: 19).

The police practice of indiscriminately stopping and questioning blacks likely deters blacks from frequenting "white" neighborhoods. Indeed, deterring

African Americans from entering specific spaces for fear of police harassment is perhaps the most effective means of perpetuating race-based territorial boundaries.

Police policies and practices that have evolved to fight the drug war have contributed significantly to the wide disparities that exist in other aspects of the criminal justice system. The statistics are sadly familiar: even though African Americans comprise only 12% of the population and approximately 13% of drug users, they constitute about 38% of all those arrested for drug offenses and about 59% of those convicted for drug offenses (Ibid.). Approximately one-third of all African-American men are under some form of criminal justice supervision. In Washington, D.C., the number is close to 50%. One unintended consequence has been the rise of African-American men who, because of felony convictions, are barred from voting. Nationwide, nearly 13% of all African American men have been disenfranchised due to felony drug convictions. In Virginia, approximately 40% of black males have lost the right to vote (Sentencing Project, 1998). Indeed, it appears that the increase in felony convictions (many for drug possession rather than sales) has inadvertently replicated the deliberate disenfranchisement affects of the Jim Crow era.

The drug war has also had a significant impact on the life chances of African Americans caught in the criminal justice juggernaut. Black males convicted of drug offenses face a less than welcoming labor market and often have difficulty finding employment after release. Together, these factors have had profoundly negative consequences for the social organization of black communities. Recycling a substantial proportion of African American males through the criminal justice system has diminished the capacity of families to remain intact, eroded community social organization, and undermined community support and confidence in the criminal justice system.

Perhaps ACLU president Ira Glasser (2000: 707) said it best when he stated, "the drug war hysteria has become an engine for the restoration of Jim Crow justice in this country." Such is the case when the policies and practices of a criminal justice system discriminate against African Americans on the basis of race.

"QUALITY OF LIFE" AND "ZERO TOLERANCE" POLICING: THE NEW BLACK CODES? (5)

In 1982, Wilson and Kelling (1982) became the standard-bearers of the current resurgence in order maintenance or "quality of life" policing with the publication of their Atlantic article, "Broken Windows." Based primarily on research conducted in Newark, New Jersey, Wilson, and Kelling argued that quality-of-life environmental factors, such as graffiti, trash, litter-filled lots, and unrepaired broken windows, as well as low-level disorderly behavior such as prostitutes gathering on corners, aggressive panhandlers, and the inebriated, were critical indicators of community disorganization and disregard. Left untended, these neighborhood conditions signaled to the criminal element that a community lacked the necessary social organization to manage its own public life, and was thus a prime target for victimization. These authors advocate assertive police order-maintenance actions to help reestablish or strengthen community behavioral norms. Although Wilson and Kelling consider the potential for inappropriate and undesirable police behavior the adoption of these practices could entail, they fail to state any possible remedies (Ibid.).

Since the publication of "Broken Windows," order maintenance or "quality of life" policing has been at the forefront of policing. In his bid for the mayor's office in New York City, Rudy Giuliani made quality of life a central point in his campaign. Upon winning the office, Giuliani tapped former Transit Chief William Bratton as Police Commissioner, who soon introduced sweeping changes to the New York Police Department (NYPD). Bratton reorganized the NYPD and introduced a computer-driven, problem-oriented internal accountability system known as COMPSTAT. He also questioned the effectiveness of the community policing practices instituted under former Mayor David Dinkins and Police Commissioner Lee Brown. Bratton refocused the police on "quality of life" offenses and advocated assertive and prominent police actions that came to be termed zero tolerance policing (ZTP).

Although it is unclear whether ZTP is true to Wilson and Kelling's original conception of Broken Windows policing, that theory has been the legitimizing premise behind the ZTP's adoption. Bratton instructed officers to crack down on squeegee men, petty drug dealers, graffiti taggers, prostitutes, and other quality-of-life offenders. Officers were encouraged and expected to assertively stop and question "suspicious persons," both to discover violations and to obtain information on other criminal activities. To empower patrol officers to address neighborhood drug problems, Bratton lifted a 20-year-old corruption-reduction reform that had banned patrol officers from engaging in drug arrests. He also created the Street Crime Units (SCU), plain clothes officers who are deployed specifically to apprehend serious offenders.

The ramifications of these new policing directives were felt most deeply by the city's minority and immigrant population. The number of minorities stopped and frisked rose precipitously with the introduction of ZTP. African Americans constitute only 25.6% of New York City's population, yet they comprised just over 50% of all persons stopped. Thirty-three percent of persons stopped were Hispanic, though they comprise only 25% of the population (Office of the New York State Attorney General [ONSAG], 1999). Nearly two-thirds of stops conducted by the SCU were of African Americans. Moreover, blacks and Hispanics were at a greater risk of being stopped in neighborhoods in which they constituted a distinct minority. In precincts in which African Americans and Hispanics constituted less than 10% of the population, they constituted 30 and 23.4% of the stops respectively. Relatively few of these stops resulted in arrest. New York police stopped 9.5 African Americans, 8.8 Hispanics, and 7.9 whites for every one arrest. The disparity is even greater for the SCU, which stopped 16.3 African Americans, 14.5 Hispanics, and 9.6 whites for every one arrest. This disparity holds even after controlling for crime rates by race (Ibid.).

Advocates of ZTP often point to the falling crime rate in New York as evidence of its effectiveness. Any analysis of the drop in crime in New York, however, must consider the range of other factors that affect crime rates, such as economic health, demographic factors, and changes in the drug economy. Recent research also questions both the causal connection between disorder and crime and the suggestion that NYPD tactics are responsible for the reduction in crime. Harcourt (1998) reexamined the original data from the Newark and Houston fear-reduction studies and found that the connection between disorder and future crime was weaker than had been previously reported. A longitudinal study of 66 Baltimore neighborhoods found that neighborhood structural factors had a greater impact on future crime than did changes in the level of "incivilities" (Taylor, 1999). Other cities, notably San Diego, have experienced drops in crime similar in magnitude to New York without adopting aggressive quality-of-life policing (Greene, 1999).

Despite evidence that questions the connection between crime and low-level disorderly behavior, many cities, citing the dramatic drop in crime in New York, have rushed to duplicate the NYPD model as the latest weapon against crime. The architects of the New York plan have built lucrative careers consulting with cities on how to implement ZTP. In Cleveland, police officers have increased the number of stops conducted sixfold in recent years (Innes, 1999). The victory of Baltimore City Council member Martin O'Malley in the city's recent mayoral race has been largely attributed to his campaigning on a "zero tolerance" on crime platform (Paik, 1999). Baltimore Police Chief Tom Frazier resigned his post rather than implement a zero tolerance plan designed by New York consultants (Rosen, 2000).

ZTP practices have also had a deleterious affect on the relationship between minorities and the police in New York. Since the implementation of ZTP, complaints against the police have risen 41%, with many of these complaints coining from people of color (Greene, 1999). However, the deaths of Amadou Diallo and Patrick Dorismond best underscore the tragic consequences of unrestrained police aggression. In February 1999, Diallo, a West African immigrant, was gunned down in the foyer of his Brooklyn apartment building by SCU officers who mistook Diallo's wallet for a gun. In the subsequent criminal trial, none of the four officers were held criminally responsible for his death. Patrick Dorismond, a security guard and the son of a Haitian official, was killed by NYPD officers running a marijuana sting when he reacted negatively to an officer's aggressive overtures to procure marijuana from him. The officers who killed Dorismond were part of a new narcotics enforcement team named "Operation Condor." Officers working in Operation Condor are required to have five narcotics arrests per shift or risk the wrath of their supervisors, a directive that likely encourages officers to engage in unnecessary stops and arrests.

Police practices to address gang violence illustrate another area in which monitoring and regulating the movements of young men of color has been a primary tactic. Gang violence has become a critical concern for law enforcement. Addressing gang violence and crime challenges fundamental principles of our legal system. While the criminal law is structured to contend with the acts of individuals, crimes committed by gang members are attributed to their group membership. Unless law enforcement agencies can find ways to tie specific individuals to a crime, they often cannot prosecute individuals they believe are tangentially involved in criminal activity. In some instances, law enforcement believes that gang violence and crime persist because individuals on the periphery of the gang protect them or enable their behavior. Further, there is a belief that preventing gang-related crimes requires the adoption of measures that destabilize gang structure and organization.

The police have developed several tools to address crimes committed by gangs. A common law enforcement tactic is the use of gang profiles. Much like drug courier profiles, gang profiles seek to delineate the distinguishing characteristics of gang members. Gang profiles focus on physical attributes and associational affiliations as indicators of gang membership. Similar to drug courier profiles, gang profiles are often a poor means for identifying gang members. Rather than a compilation of actual behaviors, gang profiles often focus on clothing, territory, identification by an informant, and affiliations. These are particularly poor measures given the widespread adoption of "gang" clothing (e.g., baggy pants, scarves, shaved heads) in popular culture and the often fluid nature of social interactions among young people.

Gang profiles are not racially neutral and these practices have led in recent years to an exponential growth in the number of young men of color identified as gang members. Nearly half of all young black men in Los Angeles County have been defined as gang members or gang associates. In Orange County, California, there are reportedly 13,609 identified gang members; approximately 75% of them are Latinos and the rest are predominantly Asian. In Denver, Colorado, two of every three young black men are on the gang list (Kim, 1996: 275). Even though white gangs are known to exist and to engage in violent and deviant acts, they are often not viewed as a problem (Ibid.). "Community opinion of white gangs...tends to be less critical than that of gangs comprised of different races" (Ibid.: 271). Hence, the definition of what constitutes a criminal gang is itself racially biased and contributes to the disproportionate number of minorities defined as gang members.

Despite the imprecision of gang profiles for identifying criminal gangs and gang members, law enforcement agencies conduct broad "sweeps" in inner-city neighborhoods using these loose criteria to identify "gang members." In many respects, these sweeps illustrate en masse the practice of indiscriminate "stopping and questioning." Many jurisdictions use this information to compile lists of "known" gang members, which law enforcement and officers of the court use. Some agencies keep photographic logs of suspected gang members. Further, states such as California have developed computerized statewide databases that list the names of known gang members. Once defined as a gang member, an individual may be eligible for enhanced penalties that may be in effect for gang-related offenses, and may have his or her movements monitored by law enforcement. The accuracy of these databases is contestable. As noted, gang profiles are a notoriously imprecise means for identifying gang members. Second, although these databases are to be purged every two years, it is unclear whether this is done on a timely basis. Indeed, the names of deceased "gang members" have appeared on a gang list years after their death. Provisions for purging the names of gang members who have left gang life are also lacking. Once someone is entered into the database, how and when his or her name will be removed is unclear.

The reliance on vague and overly broad stereotypes to identify gang members has resulted in the wholesale labeling of young men of color as gang members in some jurisdictions. In this respect, gang profiling, like other discriminatory practices, perpetuates discretionary police practices that disproportionately affect young men of color. Similar to the Black Codes of previous eras, gang profiling has developed into a system for "keeping tabs" on virtually an entire generation.

Quality-of-life policing has also been introduced to abate gang violence. Relying primarily on public nuisance laws, several jurisdictions have filed civil injunctions that severely restrict the behavior of "known" gang members in public spaces. Police and prosecutors compile extensive dossiers that document the activities of suspected gang members and their associates; depositions collected from officers and community members document the nuisance behavior of individuals. This documentation is then used to civilly enjoin specified individuals from engaging in certain behaviors in specific neighborhoods. The enjoined behaviors are typically quite extensive and cover a range of activities, including loitering in public, being seen in public with two or more known gang members, trespassing on private property without written consent of the owner, disorderly conduct, wearing "gang" clothing, violating curfews, littering, blocking free passage of streets and parks, and noise. Approximately 30 gang injunctions have been or are being filed, mostly in California. For the most part, developing case law has supported the constitutionality of the injunctions (People ex rel. Gallo v. Acuna, 1997; in re Englebrecht, 1998; Iraheta v. Superior Court of L.A. County, 1999).

Gang civil injunctions effectively bar the young men named in them from appearing in public spaces in their neighborhoods. The potential for police abuse of this extension of their discretionary power is far reaching. Officers may stop individuals indiscriminately to verify whether they are covered under the injunction agreement. As injunctions establish probable cause, enjoined individuals may be stopped at any time, regardless of whether their present behavior suggests reasonably suspicious behavior, to verify whether they are in compliance with the restrictions imposed by the injunction. Essentially, gang injunctions give police carte blanche to engage in pretextual stops of suspected gang members in specific neighborhoods.

The dangers of using civil law in lieu of criminal prosecution are substantial. For one, due process protections are attached to criminal, not civil, proceedings. Enjoined individuals have no right to counsel and must provide their own legal representation. Further, the standards of evidence are substantially lower in civil cases. This has meant that prosecutors can obtain injunctive sanctions against individuals they could not convict in criminal proceedings.

One author compared the broad reach of anti-gang civil injunctions to the vague vagrancy statutes that were part of the Black Codes (Stewart, 1998). In reviewing quality-of-life and zero tolerance policing policies and practices, the potential for police abuse of discretionary power can surely be extended to this entire genre of police behavior.

CONCLUSION

An analysis of the policies and practices associated with drug war, quality of life, and zero tolerance policing reveals a system of de facto racial discrimination driven by specific policy choices and low-level police discretionary decisions. The subtlety of these forms of discrimination makes it difficult to offer definitive solutions. Since many of these polices are racially neutral on their face, the victims are obliged to prove racial bias and discrimination. To date, there does not appear to be strong legal grounds for using racially disparate impact as an indicator of racially discriminatory policies (e.g., McCleskey v. Kemp, 1987). Thus, even as the number of young men of color detained, harassed, profiled, labeled, or arrested continues to escalate, few in policymaking positions question whether the fundamental premises of policy choices portend racially skewed outcomes.

Exposing bias in police discretionary decisions may be even more difficult. Since these practices involve low-level discretionary behavior that often occurs beyond the purview of the public, concrete evidence of bias is often elusive. In an effort to quantify possible racial bias in traffic stops, several police departments have voluntarily begun to collect data on all traffic stops. Such local efforts are a positive step toward obtaining substantiating evidence, but in the absence of standardized, nationwide data-collection requirements, local data collection systems are of varying depth and quality.

Should the data demonstrate racial bias, intent must often also be established for these practices to be deemed legally discriminatory. The standard of intent presumes that officers are conscious of their racially biased behavior. Although some officers clearly may be, the centrality of racial bias in the development of policing suggests that individual intent is not a necessary precursor to race-based decision-making. Indeed, when an institution has developed within a racially discriminatory social and political environment, when racial social control has historically been a fundamental function of that institution, and when guiding public policies and the informal social system support racial bias, racial discrimination is likely to be an inherent part of its organizing ethos. Our search for the intentional "racist" moment when an officer deliberately chooses to treat someone differently due to race misses the broader social, political, and organizational cues that instruct officer behavior. Moreover, focusing on individual intent rather than on institutional imperatives limits the discussion to individually focused solutions, such as narrowly construed cultural sensitivity training and individual disciplinary actions, rather than solutions that seek to transform institutions and organizations more generally.

Change can be accomplished; however, it requires a more thoughtful consideration of the broader factors that affect police organizations and police work. For example, policies that seek to forward broader social justice ends— drug treatment instead of incarceration, scattered site housing rather than concentrated ghettos, community capacity building and economic development, job training, and early childhood and youth development—can ultimately change the environment in which the police operate and thus may in the long term lead to a rethinking of policing strategies.

Change in police organizations is also required. Although evaluations of community-policing programs report mixed results, this may reflect the narrow design of many programs. Community-policing rhetoric often waxes poetic about interagency collaboration and community partnership; however, few programs fully embrace these ends. In many cities, community-policing programs are defined, organized, and implemented by the police themselves. Perhaps a better approach would be to view community policing as a precursor to community-oriented government more generally. Community-oriented governments in which governing structures support community participation and relevant city agencies receive adequate resources to work collaboratively with the police toward the larger goal of community restoration would likely result in a model of policing that differs substantially from most current programs that often ask police officers to act as community mobilizers, organizers, advocates, and enforcers. Under a community-oriented government scheme, a city experiencing problems with gang membership might pursue gang outreach, youth development programs, job training, educational support, diversion to counseling or treatment, and law enforcement as a complete policy response.

Moreover, a fundamental shift must take place in the way the police envision their role in a multicultural democracy. Police must work toward building an organizational infrastructure that supports diversity within the organization and recognizes the challenges of serving a diverse population. For example, an organization committed to diversity would develop organizational measures for evaluating progress. Standard measures would include the number of racial minority and women officers, the quantity of cultural diversity training hours, and community surveys. Departments would develop measures for assessing recruitment and retention programs, officer attitudes and departmental climate, and complaints from Internal Affairs, and also set up a citizen review body and document and analyze field interrogation, Terry stop, and traffic stop data. Further, departments would not rely solely on managerial staff or in-house analysts to review this data. Rather, the department could establish a diversity community council made up of community members who would review the department's progress and issue annual diversity report cards. Collecting and analyzing these types of qualitative and quantitative measurements would more accurately assess how a department was performing with regard to diversity. Moreover, it would send a strong message that respect for diversity within the organization and the broader community was supported at the highest levels of the department. Clearly, these suggestions are far more comprehensive than those typically pursued. Implementing changes like these would require us to go beyond the narrow solutions typically offered when considering police reform and to embark on developing police organizations that are truly prepared to protect and serve the multicultural reality in which we all live.

Sandra Bass, Ph.D., is Assistant Professor at the University of Maryland, Department of Criminology and Government and Politics (2220 Le Frak Hall, College Park, MD 20742; e-mail: sbass@crim.umd.edu).

NOTES

1.   For example, Massey and Denton (1993) extensively discuss how federal highway and FHA policy encouraged racial segregation.

2.   Sugrue (1996: 252–253) recounts the normal course of protest activities in this excerpt. "Demonstrations followed a predictable pattern. Early in the evening, community members would drive slowly in the vicinity of a newly purchased black home, beckoning neighbors to join the protest. Crowds gathered after the dinner hour, drawing men who had just returned home from work, and school-age children, especially teenagers, who played in the streets in the evening. Often outdoor protests followed emergency improvement association meetings. Mob activity ranged from milling about in front of targeted houses, to shouting racial epithets, to throwing stones and bricks. The intensity of violence in the early stages depended on the presence of the police. Frequently officers were slow to respond to housing incidents, and residents had ample time to hurl objects at the offending houses. After police arrived, they often passively watched crowds gather, without dispersing them for parading without a permit, disorderly conduct, or riot. When the police broke up crowds for obstructing traffic or for crowding the sidewalk, smaller groups usually reconstituted themselves on neighbors' lawns and porches, safe havens from the police who did not venture onto private property to control crowds. From the sanctuary of nearby yards, enraged neighbors continued to taunt their new black neighbors, to shout their disapproval at the police, and to throw cans, stones, or bottles toward the targeted house."

3.   In 1910, African American home-owning rates were among the highest in the country at 36%. Only 2.4% of African Americans owned their homes in New York (Laslet, 1996; Bunch, 1990: 103).

4.   I am indebted to Ira Glasser (2000) for making this analogy.

5.   I am indebted to Gary Stewart (1998) for this analogy.

REFERENCES

Anderson, Elijah. 1990. Streetwise. Chicago: University of Chicago Press.

Blauner, Robert. 1969. "Internal Colonialism and Ghetto Revolt." Social Problems 16 (Spring).

Bunch, Lonnie, III. 1990. "A Past Not Necessarily Prologue: The Afro-American in Los Angeles Since 1900." Norman Klein and Martin Schiesl (eds.), 20th Century Los Angeles: Power, Promotion, and Social Conflict. Claremont: Regina Books.

Chambliss, William. 1994. "Policing the Ghetto Underclass." Social Problems (May).

Cho, Sumi. 1993. "Korean Americans and African Americans: Conflict and Construction." Robert Gooding-Williams (ed.), Reading Rodney King/Reading Urban Uprising. New York: Routledge.

Cole, David. 1999. No Equal Justice: Race and Class in the American Criminal Justice System. New York: New Press.

de Toqueville, Alexis. 2000. Democracy in America, Volume II. (First published 1835.) New York: Bantam Books.

Escobar, Edward. 1999. Race, Police, and the Making of a Political Identity: Mexican Americans and the Los Angeles Police Department, 1900–1945. Berkeley: University of California Press.

Franklin, John Hope and Loren Schweninger. 1999. Runaway Slaves: Rebels on the Plantation 1790–1860. Oxford: Oxford University Press.

Friedman, Lawrence. 1981. The Roots of Justice: Crime and Punishment in Alameda County, California 1870–1910. Chapel Hill: University of North Carolina Press.

Glasser, Ira. 2000. "American Drug Laws: The New Jim Crow. The 1999 Edward C. Sobota Lecture." Albany Law Review 63:703.

Greene, Judith. 1999. "Zero Tolerance: A Case Study of Police Policies and Practices in New York City." Crime and Delinquency 45, 2.

Hall, Stuart et al. 1978. Policing the Crisis: Mugging, the State, and Law and Order. London: Macmillan.

Harcourt, Bernard. 1998. "Reflecting on the Subject: A Critique of the Social Influence Conception of Deterrence, the Broken Windows Theory, and Order Maintenance Policing New York Style." Michigan Law Review 97 (November): 291.

Harris, David. 1999. "The Stories, the Statistics, and the Law: Why Driving While Black Matters." Minnesota Law Review 84:265.

Herbert, Steve. 1997. Policing Space: Territoriality and the Los Angeles Police Department. Minneapolis: University of Minnesota Press.

Innes, Martin. 1999. "An Iron Fist in an Iron Glove? The Zero Tolerance Policing Debate." The Howard Journal 38,4 (November).

Kim, Suzin. 1996. "Gangs Anti Law Enforcement: The Necessity of Limiting the Use of Gang Profiles." The Boston Public Interest Low Journal (Winter).

Laslet, John H. M. 1996. "Historical Perspectives: Immigration and the Rise of a Distinctive Urban Region, 1900–1970." Roger Waldinger and Mehdi Bozorgmehr (eds.), Ethnic Los Angeles. New York: Russell Sage Foundation.

Massey, Douglas S. and Nancy A. Denton. 1993. American Apartheid: Segregation and the Making of the Underclass. Cambridge: Harvard University Press.

Mirande, Alfredo. 1987. Gringo Justice. Notre Dame, IN: University of Notre Dame Press.

Myrdal, Gunnar. 1944. An American Dilemma: The Negro Problem and Modern Democracy. New York: Harper and Row.

Office of the New York State Attorney General (ONSAG). 1999. "The New York City Police Department's 'Stop and Frisk' Practices: A Report to the People of the State of New York from the Office of the Attorney General, Civil Rights Bureau." (December 1).

Paik, Angela. 1999. "Zero Tolerance Strikes a Chord: Anti-Crime Message Works for Baltimore Nominee." Washington Post (September 16): B-1.

Platt, Anthony M. et al. 1982. The Iron Fist and the Velvet Glove. San Francisco, CA: Global Options.

Reichel, Philip L. 1999. "Southern Slave Patrols as a Transitional Police Type." Policing Perspectives: An Anthology. Los Angeles: Roxbury Publishing Company.

Rosen, Jeffery. 2000. "A Look At…Zero Tolerance: When Good Policing Goes Bad." Washington Post (April 23): B-3.

Russell, Katheryn K. 1998. The Color of Crime: Racial Hoaxes, White Fear, Black Protectionism, Police Harassment, and Other Macroaggressions. New York: New York University Press.

Schiesl, Martin. 1990. "Beyond the Badge." Norman Klein and Martin Schiesl (eds.), 20th Century Los Angeles: Power, Promotion, and Social Conflict. Claremont: Regina Books.

Sentencing Project. 1998. Losing the Vote: The Impact of Felony Disenfranchisement Laws in the United States. Washington, D.C.: The Sentencing Project.

Staples, Robert. 2001. "White Racism, Black Crime, and American Justice: An Application of the Colonial Model to Explain Crime and Race." David V. Barker and Richard P. Davin (eds.), Crime, Criminology, and Criminal Justice. Guilford: CT: McGraw-Hill/Dushkin (reprinted from Phylon 1972).

Stewart, Gary. 1998. "Black Codes and Broken Windows: The Legacy of Racial Hegemony in Anti-Gang Civil Injunctions." Yale Law Journal (May).

Sugrue, Thomas J. 1996. The Origins of the Urban Crisis: Race and Inequality in Postwar Detroit. Princeton: Princeton University Press.

Taylor, Ralph B. 1999. "Crime, Grime, Fear, and Decline: A Longitudinal Look." National Institute of Justice, Research in Brief (July).

United States Commission on Civil Rights. 1999. Racial and Ethnic Tensions in American Communities: Poverty, Inequality, and Discrimination. Volume V: The Los Angeles Report. Washington, D.C. 1970. Mexican Americans and the Administration of Justice in the Southwest. Washington, D.C.

Williams, Hubert and Patrick Murphy. 1990. "The Evolving Strategy of the Police: A Minority View." Victor Kappeler (ed.), The Police and Society. Illinois: Waveland Press.

Wilson, James Q. and George Kelling. 1982. "Broken Windows: The Police and Neighborhood Safety." The Atlantic: 249 (March).

Woodward, C. Vann. 1968. The Strange Career of Jim Crow. London: Oxford University Press.

WPA Slave Narratives Project. 2001. Andy Anderson ex-slave, in Been Here So Long—Selections from the WPA Slave Narratives Project. http://newdeal.feri.org/asn/asn12.htm, accessed 05/09/2001.

Zhao, Jihong. 1996. Why Police Organizations Change: A Study of Community-Oriented Policing. Police Executive Research Forum, Washington, D.C.

CASES CITED

1997. People ex rel. Gallo v. Acuna. Supreme Court of California, 14 Cal. 4th 1090; 929 P2d 596.

1998. In re Englebrecht. Court of Appeal of California, Fourth Appellate District, Division One, 67 Cal. App. 4th 486.

1999. Iraheta v. Superior Court of LA. County. Court of Appeal of California, Second Appellate District, Division Two, 70 Cal. App. 4th 1500.

1987. McCleskey v. Kemp 481 U.S. 279.

War on Terror

4

Flying While Arab: Lessons from the Racial Profiling Controversy

David Harris

I n the aftermath of the September 11 tragedies in New York and Washington, DC, we Americans have heard countless times that our country has "changed forever." In many ways, especially in terms of national and personal security, this is quite true. Americans have always assumed that terrorism and other violent manifestations of the world's problems did not and would never happen here, that our geographic isolation by the Atlantic and Pacific Oceans protected us. Indeed, since the Civil War, the United States has experienced no sustained violence or war on its own soil. Sadly, we know now that we are vulnerable, and that like countries all over the world, we must take steps to protect ourselves.

This is the new reality that Americans find themselves adjusting to: searches and inspections of ourselves and our belongings when we enter public buildings and areas, such as government offices, sports stadiums, and airport concourses; increased presence of law enforcement and even military personnel; enhanced police powers and curtailed civil liberties; and new powers and tactics our government will use to deal more strictly with foreigners and immigrants. While some of these changes amount to little more than inconveniences, others—particularly changes in the law that limit individual freedom while expanding government power—are in fact major changes in our way of

"Flying while Arab: Lessons from the racial profiling controversy," by David Harris from *Civil Rights Journal,* 2002. Copyright 2002, U. S. Commission on Civil Rights.

life and the core values and meaning of American society. The U.S. Congress has already passed a sweeping piece of legislation, increasing government power over everything from wiretaps, e-mail, formerly secret grand jury information, to the detention and trial of noncitizens.

We know that the United States is a nation of immigrants—that, in many ways, immigrants built our great nation. We know that the immigrant experience has, in many ways, been at the core of the American experience, along with the experiences of African Americans liberated from slavery. The diversity and energy that immigrants have brought to our country has been, and continues to be, one of our greatest strengths. But, we also know that we have sometimes dealt harshly and unfairly with immigrants and noncitizen residents, especially in times of national emergency and crisis. Thus, it is critical that we try to understand the implications of the changes that have taken place and will continue because of the events of September 11—changes in the very idea of what America is, and in what it will be in the future.

One of these changes has been particularly noticeable—both because it represents a radical shift in what we did prior to September 11, and because it also continues a public discussion that was taking place in our country before that terrible day. Racial profiling—the use of race or ethnic appearance as a factor in deciding who merits police attention as a suspicious person—has undergone a sudden and almost complete rehabilitation. Prior to September 11, many Americans had recognized racial profiling for what it is—a form of institutional discrimination that had gone unquestioned for too long. Thirteen states had passed anti-profiling bills of one type or another, and hundreds of police departments around the country had begun to collect data on all traffic stops, in order to facilitate better, unbiased practices. On the federal level, Congressman John Conyers, Jr., of Michigan and Senator Russell Feingold of Wisconsin had introduced the End Racial Profiling Act of 2001, a bill aimed at directly confronting and reducing racially biased traffic stops through a comprehensive, management-based, carrot-and-stick approach.

September 11 dramatically recast the issue of racial profiling. Suddenly, racial profiling was not a discredited law enforcement tactic that alienated and injured citizens while it did little to combat crime and drugs; instead, it became a vital tool to assure national security, especially in airports. The public discussion regarding the targets of profiling changed too—from African Americans, Latinos, and other minorities suspected of domestic crime, especially drug crime, to Arab Americans, Muslims, and others of Middle Eastern origin, who looked like the suicidal hijackers of September 11. In some respects, this was not hard to understand. The September 11 attacks had caused catastrophic damage and loss of life among innocent civilians; people were shocked, stunned, and afraid. And they knew that all of the hijackers were Arab or Middle Eastern men carrying out the deadly threats of Osama bin Laden's al Qaeda terrorist network based in the Middle East, which of course claims Islam as its justification for the attacks and many others around the world. Therefore, many said that it just makes sense to profile people who looked

Arab, Muslim, or Middle Eastern. After all, "they" were the ones who'd carried out the attacks and continued to threaten us; ignoring these facts amounted to some kind of political correctness run amok in a time of great danger.

But if the renewed respectability and use of profiling was one of the ways in which September 11 changed things, we might also notice that the "new" racial profiling demonstrated the truth of an old saw: the more things change, the more they stay the same. We should remember that racial profiling of African Americans and Latinos also originated in a war—the metaphorical "war on drugs"—and was justified with the same arguments. But even more importantly, we should learn from what we now know were the grand mistakes of profiling in the last 10 years. If we do that, we will see that using Arab or Muslim background or appearance to profile for potential terrorists will almost certainly fail—even as it damages our enforcement efforts and our capacity to collect intelligence.

HISTORY

As in almost any serious policy inquiry, a look at the history of our country can help us attain a proper perspective on how to view what we do now. Unfortunately, that history gives us reasons to feel concern at this critical juncture. Any serious appraisal of American history during some of the key periods of the 20th century would counsel an abundance of caution; when we have faced other national security crises, we have sometimes overreacted—or at the very least acted more out of emotion than was wise.

In the wake of World War I, the infamous Palmer Raids resulted in the rounding up of a considerable number of immigrants. These people were deported, often without so much as a scintilla of evidence. During World War II, tens of thousands of Japanese—immigrants and native born, citizens and legal residents—were interned in camps, their property confiscated and sold off at fire-sale prices. To its everlasting shame, the U.S. Supreme Court gave the internment of the Japanese its constitutional blessing in the infamous Korematsu case. It took the United States government decades, but eventually it apologized and paid reparations to the Japanese. And during the 1950s, the Red Scare resulted in the mining of lives and careers and the jailing of citizens, because they had had the temerity to exercise their constitutionally protected rights to free association by becoming members of the Communist Party years or even decades before.

Hopefully, we can see the common thread that runs through these now notorious examples: an apprehension of danger to the country not only from the outside but from a group of people within who are identified racially, ethnically, or politically with those thought to pose the threat, and a willingness to take measures that sweep widely through the identified group—more widely than the threat might justify. (Of course, we have also learned that these threats have been wildly exaggerated; for example, the discovery of government documents more than four decades after the internment of the Japanese showed that the government misled the courts by intentionally withholding critical information that contradicted official efforts to make the case for a sufficiently severe threat to justify the internment. (1)) The threat we face now bears many similarities: a danger from overseas posed by one group, and an identified group in the United States that has come under suspicion. All of this ought to encourage us not to leap forward with racial or ethnic profiling, but to hesitate before we do.

CATEGORICAL THINKING

We must hope that we have learned the lessons of this history—that the emotions of the moment, when we feel threatened, can cause us to damage our civil liberties and our fellow citizens, particularly our immigrant populations. And it is this legacy that should make us think now, even as we engage in a long and detailed investigation of the September 11 terror attacks. As we listen to accounts of that investigation, reports indicate that the investigation has been strongly focused on Arab Americans and Muslims. What's more, private citizens have made Middle Eastern appearance an important criterion in deciding how to react to those who look different around them. Many of these reports have involved treatment of persons of Middle Eastern descent in airports.

In itself, this is not really surprising. We face a situation in which there has been a terrorist attack by a small group of suicidal hijackers, and as far as we know, all of those involved were Arabs and Muslims and had Arabic surnames. Some or all had entered the country recently. Given the incredibly high stakes, some Americans have reacted to Middle Easterners as a group, based on their appearance. In a way, this is understandable. We seldom have much information on any of the strangers around us, so we tend to think in broad categories like race and gender. When human beings experience fear, it is a natural reaction to make judgments concerning our safety based on these broad categories, and to avoid those who arouse fear in us. This may translate easily into a type of racial and ethnic profiling, in which—as has been reported—passengers on airliners refuse to fly with other passengers who have a Middle Eastern appearance.

USE OF RACE AND ETHNIC APPEARANCE
IN LAW ENFORCEMENT

The far more worrying development, however, is the possibility that profiling of Arabs and Muslims will become standard procedure in law enforcement. Again, it is not hard to understand the impulse; we want to catch and stop these suicidal hijackers, every one of whom fits the description of Arab or Muslim. So we stop, question, and search more of these people because we believe it's a way to play the odds. If all the September 11 terrorists were Middle Easterners, then we get the biggest bang for the enforcement buck by questioning, searching, and screening as many Middle Easterners as possible. This should, we think, give us the best chance of finding those who helped the terrorists or those bent on creating further havoc.

But we need to be conscious of some of the things that we have learned over the last few years in the ongoing racial profiling controversy. Using race or ethnic appearance as part of a description of particular suspects may indeed help an investigation; using race or ethnic appearance as a broad predictor of who is involved in crime or terrorism will likely hurt our investigative efforts. All the evidence indicates that profiling Arab Americans or Muslims would be an ineffective waste of law enforcement resources that would damage our intelligence efforts while it compromises basic civil liberties. If we want to do everything we can to secure our country, we have to be smart about the steps we take.

As we think about the possible profiling of Arabs and Muslims, recall the arguments made for years about domestic efforts against drugs and crime. African Americans and Latinos are disproportionately involved in drug crime, proponents of profiling said; therefore concentrate on them. Many state and local police agencies, led by the federal Drug Enforcement Administration, did exactly that from the late 1980s on. We now know that police departments in many jurisdictions used racial profiling, especially in efforts to get drugs and guns off the highways and out of the cities. For example, state police in Maryland used a profile on Interstate 95 during the 1990s in an effort to apprehend drug couriers. According to data from the state police themselves, while only 17 percent of the drivers on the highway were African American, over 70 percent of those stopped and searched were black. Statistics from New Jersey, New York, and other jurisdictions showed similar patterns: the only factor that predicted who police stopped and searched was race or ethnicity. (2) No other factor—not driving behavior, not the crime rate of an area or neighborhood, and not reported crimes that involved persons of particular racial or ethnic groups—explained the outcomes that showed great racial or ethnic disproportionalities among those stopped and searched.

But as we look back, what really stands out is how ineffective this profile-based law enforcement was. If proponents of profiling were right—that police should concentrate on minorities because criminals were disproportionately minorities—focusing on "those people" should yield better returns on the investment of law enforcement resources in crime fighting than traditional policing does. In other words, using profiles that include racial and ethnic appearance should succeed more often than enforcement based on other, less sophisticated techniques. In any event, it should not succeed less often than traditional policing. But in fact, in departments that focused on African Americans, Latinos, and other minorities, the "hit rates"—the rates of searches that succeeded in finding contraband like drugs or guns—were actually lower for minorities than were the hit rates for whites, who of course were not apprehended by using a racial or ethnic profile. That's right: when police agencies used race or ethnic appearance as a factor—not as the only factor but one factor among many—they did not get the higher returns on their enforcement efforts that they were expecting. Instead, they did not do as well; their use of traditional police methods against whites did a better job than racial profiling, and did not sweep a high number of innocent people into law enforcement's net.

The reason that this happened is subtle but important: race and ethnic appearance are very poor predictors of behavior. Race and ethnicity describe people well, and there is absolutely nothing wrong with using skin color or other features to describe known suspects. But since only a very small percentage of African Americans and Latinos participate in the drug trade, race and ethnic appearance do a bad job identifying the particular African Americans and Latinos in whom police should be interested. Racial and ethnic profiling caused police to spread their enforcement activities far too widely and indiscriminately. The results of this misguided effort have been disastrous for law enforcement. This treatment has alienated African Americans, Latinos, and other minorities from the police—a critical strategic loss in the fight against crime, since police can only win this fight if they have the full cooperation and support of those they serve. And it is precisely this lesson we ought to think about now, as the cry goes up to use profiling and intensive searches against people who look Arab, Middle Eastern, or Muslim.

PROFILING TO CATCH TERRORISTS

Using race, ethnic appearance, or religion as a way to decide who to regard as a potential terrorist will almost surely produce the same kinds of results: no effect on terrorist activity; many innocent people treated like suspects; damage to our enforcement and prevention efforts.

Even if the suicide hijackers of September 11 shared a particular ethnic appearance or background, subjecting all Middle Easterners to intrusive questioning, stops, or searches will have a perverse and unexpected effect: it will spread our enforcement and detection efforts over a huge pool of people who police would not otherwise think worthy of attention. The vast majority of people who look like Mohammed Atta and the other hijackers will never have anything to do with any kind of ethnic or religious extremism. Yet a profile that includes race, ethnicity, or religion may well include them, drawing them into the universe of people who law enforcement will stop, question, and search. Almost all of them will be people who would not otherwise have attracted police attention, because no other aspect of their behavior would have drawn scrutiny. Profiling will thus drain enforcement efforts and resources away from more worthy investigative efforts and tactics that focus on the close observation of behavior—like the buying of expensive one-way tickets with cash just a short time before takeoff, as some of the World Trade Center hijackers did.

This has several important implications. First, just as happened with African Americans and Latinos in the war on drugs, profiling of Arabs and Muslims will be overinclusive—it will put many more under police suspicion of terrorist activity than would otherwise be warranted. Almost all of these people will be hard-working, tax-paying, law-abiding individuals. While they might understand one such stop to be a mere inconvenience that they must put up with for the sake of national security, repetition of these experiences for large numbers of people within the same ethnic groups will lead to resentment, alienation, and anger at the authorities.

Second, and perhaps more important, focusing on race and ethnicity keeps police attention on a set of surface details that tells us very little and draws officers' attention away from what is much more important and concrete: behavior. The two most important tools law enforcement agents have in preventing crime and catching criminals are observation of behavior and intelligence. As any experienced police officer knows, what's important in understanding who's up to no good is not what people look like, but what they do. Investigating people who "look suspicious" will often lead officers down the wrong path; the key to success is to observe behavior. Anyone who simply looks different may seem strange or suspicious to the untrained eye; the veteran law enforcement officer knows that suspicious behavior is what really should attract attention and investigation. Thus focusing on those who "look suspicious" will necessarily take police attention away from those who act suspicious. Even in the current climate, in which we want to do everything possible to prevent another attack and to apprehend those who destroyed the World Trade Center and damaged the Pentagon, law enforcement resources are not infinite. We Americans must make decisions on how we run our criminal investigation and prevention efforts that move us away from doing just anything, and toward doing what is most effective.

Third, if observation of suspicious behavior is one of law enforcement's two important tools, using profiles of Arabs, Muslims, and other Middle Easterners can damage our capacity to make use of the other tool: the gathering, analysis, and use of intelligence. There is nothing exotic about intelligence; it simply means information that can be useful in crime fighting. If we are concerned about terrorists of Middle Eastern origin, among the most fertile places from which to gather intelligence will be the Arab American and Muslim communities. If we adopt a security policy that stigmatizes every member of these groups in airports and other public places with intrusive stops, questioning, and searches, we will alienate them from the enforcement efforts at precisely the time we need them most. And the larger the population we subject to this treatment, the greater the total amount of damage we inflict on law-abiding persons.

And of course the profiling of Arabs and Muslims assumes that we need worry about only one type of terrorist. We must not forget that, prior to the attacks on September 11, the most deadly terrorist attack on American soil was carried out not by Middle Easterners with Arabic names and accents, but by two very average American white men: Timothy McVeigh, a U.S. Army veteran from upstate New York, and Terry Nichols, a farmer from Michigan. Yet we were smart enough in the wake of McVeigh and Nichols' crime not to call for a profile emphasizing the fact that the perpetrators were white males. The unhappy truth is that we just don't know what the next group of terrorists might look like.

RACE OR ETHNICITY AS JUST ONE FACTOR AMONG MANY?

In many discussions of profiling, the question some raise is not whether to use race or ethnic appearance, but how. Proponents and defenders of racial and ethnic profiling have argued that profiling would be both acceptable and effective if race or ethnic appearance was not the only factor that indicated suspicion, but just one factor among many. The idea is that race and ethnic appearance should never be the only factors that prompt suspicion, but could be useful if they are part of the whole picture that also includes behavior. Are there, in fact, conditions under which it might make sense to treat people differently according to their race or ethnic appearance, as long as it is just one factor among many?

Our prior experience with profiling counsels against this approach. Despite what many believe, racial profiling has almost never involved situations in which police used race as the only factor in deciding which drivers or pedestrians to stop. In fact, it would be surprising if this were ever true. Human motivation is far too complex in any given situation to be based on one fact; moreover, even the thickest, most bigoted member of a police organization would know better than to simply stop people based on race. And the numbers of drivers and pedestrians in the world would make this impossible anyway; as Justice Robert Jackson said many years ago, when he was the attorney general of the U.S., traffic laws and violators of those laws are so numerous that police must inevitably choose between violators when deciding against whom to enforce the law.

But even if race or ethnicity is just one factor among others, it still presents dangers. Using race or ethnicity for purposes other than describing a particular suspect or suspects means that we must accept that race or ethnicity can become the dominant or most important factor among all of the others. And since people remain likely to attribute suspicion to those different from themselves in the broad categorical ways discussed earlier, we end up with race or ethnicity not just as an additional, sharpening factor as we focus suspicion, but as the factor that for all practical purposes directs our actions as we decide who to stop, question, and search. This, of course, brings us back to the pillars of traditional policing: race or ethnic appearance may be a valuable descriptor, but it is not behavior. It tells us nothing about what people do or have done, and instead distracts us from observing behavior.

Second, we cannot discount the obvious skill and determination of the adversaries we face in this struggle. The September 11 attacks made clear that the al Qaeda terrorists were not wild, unguided fanatics. Rather they showed a high degree of intelligence and cunning, spotting and taking advantage of unnoticed weaknesses in our immigration and aviation security systems. They showed the ability and the patience for long-range planning and careful action, as well as strict self-discipline. All of this is, of course, in addition to a belief in their own cause so strong that they were willing to sacrifice their own lives to attain their goals. And we cannot forget that the attack on the World Trade Center on September 11 was not the first, but the second attempt to destroy those buildings; their first attempt, in 1993, was unsuccessful, and they watched, waited, and planned for eight years to try again. With enemies of such craftiness and determination, it seems extremely unlikely that they will use people for their next attack who look like exactly what we are looking for. Rather, they will shift to light-skinned people who look less like Arabs or Middle Easterners, without Arabic names, or to people who are not Middle Easterners at all, such as individuals from African nations or the Philippines. (In both places, there are significant numbers of Muslims, a small but significant number of whom have been radicalized.) This, of course, will put us back where we started, and racial or ethnic appearance will become a longest-of-longshot, almost certainly an ineffective predictor at best, and a damaging distracting factor at worst.

CONCLUSION

The terrorist attacks in New York and Washington, DC, present us with many difficult choices that will test us. We will have to ask ourselves deep questions: Who are we, as a nation? What is important to us? What values lay at the core of our Constitution and our democracy? How will we find effective ways to secure ourselves without giving up what is best about our country? The proper balance between safety and civil rights will sometimes be difficult to see. But we should not simply repeat the mistakes of the past as we take on this new challenge. Only our adversaries would gain from that.

David Harris is Balk Professor of Law and Values at the University of Toledo College of Law, and Soros Senior Justice Fellow. He is the author of Profiles in Injustice: Why Racial Profiling Cannot Work, The New Press, 2002.

REFERENCES

1. See Korematsu v. United States 584 F. Supp. 1406 (N.D. Cal. 1984); Hirabayashi v. United States, 627 E Supp. 1445 (W.D. Wash. 1986), aff'd in part and rev'd in part, 828 F.2d 591 (9th Circuit, 1987).

2. For Maryland numbers, see John Lamberth, testimony before the Congressional Black Caucus, 1998, accessed at www.lamberthconsulting.com/downloads/cbc_presentation.doc; see also Wilkins v. Maryland State Police, No. CCB-93-468 (order of Apr. 22, 1997) and Maryland State Conference of NAACP Branches, et al. v. Maryland Department of State Polic, et al., 72 F.Supp 2d 560 (September 1999). For New Jersey, see John Lamberth, "Revised Statistical Analysis of the Incidence of Police Stops and Arrests of Black Drivers/Travelers on the New Jersey Turnpike Between Exits or Interchanges 1 and 3 from the Years 1988 through 1991." November 1994, accessed at www.lamberthconsulting.com/research_articles.asp. For New York, see Eliot Spitzer, Attorney General of the State of New York, "The New York Police Department's 'Stop and Frisk' Practices: A Report to the People of the State of New York," 1999, accessed at www.oag.state.ny.us/press/reports/stop_frisk/stp_frsk.pdf.

5

Last Week, Profiling Was Wrong (After the Attacks) (Column)

Joyce Purnick

Just a week ago, it seemed so simple, so universally accepted that it had become the received wisdom. Racial profiling was wrong. The mayor of New York said the city never engaged in it; the men running to succeed him denounced it.

But that was then and this is now, after the terrorist assault on Tuesday that changed and confused everything. It doesn't seem simple anymore, the question of racial profiling. Is it O.K. now—even necessary—to stereotype in a city that has become a prime target of terrorists?

That question is not theoretical. At checkpoints set up at bridges into Manhattan this week, some drivers said that officers seemed to single out drivers who appeared to be Arabs or Muslims. (The officers said no, they stopped cars at random.)

Thursday night at Kennedy International Airport, witnesses said that officers looking for people connected to the terrorist attacks were selective about whom they searched. "Anyone with dark skin or who spoke with an accent was taken aside and searched," one passenger said. "And then they went to any male with too much facial hair."

That sure sounds like profiling—directed at Muslims or Arabs rather than at blacks and Latinos, the more likely targets of profiling in New York, but profiling nonetheless.

That passenger's quotation, from an article that appeared in The New York Times yesterday, caught the attention of Zaheer Ali, a graduate student at Columbia University. "Given the recent debate on racial profiling, I wonder what folks think of this?" he asked in a message to an e-mail discussion group yesterday.

"Is it O.K. since it's designed to protect us? Is this the same rationale used by police when practicing it in our community?"

Mr. Ali, who describes himself as black, Asian and Muslim, said subsequently over the phone that he had decided it was not O.K. "I've faced both kinds of profiling driving while black and flying while Muslim," said the 28-year-old student. "If we get to the point where we begin curbing our civil liberties and the rights of certain people, I think the terrorists have won."

The thought is generous. It sounds like what the best of New York wants to be. But is it naive? We asked the candidates for mayor, all critics of racial profiling. Each suspended campaigning after Tuesday's attacks, but most agreed to talk about the issue yesterday, perhaps recognizing that it is central to the city's identity. Two declined comment: Alan G. Hevesi, who discussed other problems New Yorkers are facing but said he'd rather not talk about security. And Michael R. Bloomberg, who would not come to the telephone even to say he had no comment, leaving that to a spokesman.

Among the four other main candidates in the Democratic and Republican primaries, only Fernando Ferrer sounded as he might have before Tuesday's destruction of the twin towers. "There needs to be reasonable cause in all cases," he said, explaining when he thinks it is acceptable to stop and search people. "We've got to be very careful as Americans not to toss our values out the window, especially at moments like this. That doesn't mean we let our guard down on terrorism. But the point here is who we are as people."

Mark Green said: "During the equivalent of a state of emergency, I'm not prepared to second-guess antiterrorist security measures. Racial profiling is wrong, no matter whom it is imposed against. You need reasonable grounds. But El Al might, rationally, not interview an 80-year-old grandma for as long as they interview a young, stockier person before the plane takes off."

He added, "We can't let terrorists turn us into them."

Peter F. Vallone, who is not campaigning but manages to stand next to Mayor Rudolph W. Giuliani at briefings (which gets him on camera), questioned definitions. "It isn't racial profiling, it's identification," he said of recent actions by the authorities. "They have a list of dozens of known terrorists with descriptions. That's what they are looking for."

But where is the line? If the authorities are looking for a dark-complexioned man, do officers stop every man with a dark complexion? In New York City?

Herman Badillo, Mr. Bloomberg's rival for the Republican nomination, said: "In times of war, too far is never too far. The first thing is to protect the population, and you cannot worry about people being concerned about being racially profiled."

But does a free society then become, as Mr. Green cautioned, like the totalitarian countries that produce twisted people who murder thousands of innocents?

No, this is not a simple matter. Not simple at all.

6

Though Not Linked to Terrorism, Many Detainees Cannot Go Home (Arabs and Muslims under Deportation Orders in the U.S.)

Christopher Drew and Judith Miller

The Justice Department has blocked the departures of 87 foreign detainees who had been ordered deported or had agreed to go home, while investigators comb through information pouring in from overseas to ensure that they have no ties to terrorism, law enforcement officials say.

Most of the detainees are Arabs or Muslims, and many have spent more than 100 days in jail waiting to leave the country, with no end to detention in sight. Nearly all were jailed after being picked up on visa violations at traffic stops or because of neighbors' suspicions.

Officials said available evidence suggested they had played no role in the Sept. 11 attacks or Osama bin Laden's Al Qaeda network, and the immigration cases against some of them were resolved as long as four months ago.

They have nonetheless been held in an unusual legal limbo while investigators check their backgrounds and new evidence about Al Qaeda and other terrorist groups emerging from Afghanistan and other countries.

In the past, visa violators who had no other charges against them were usually deported or allowed to leave voluntarily 60 to 90 days after their immigration cases were closed, lawyers said. But these detainees are being treated differently.

American officials acknowledged a great reluctance to release people who could be involved with terrorism and said that the Federal Bureau of Investigation was working hard to complete the checks.

"We have to be very careful about the people we let go," said a senior Justice Department official, who spoke on condition of not being identified by name.

Civil liberties advocates agreed that the government needed to be careful but said the delays were stretching the normal legal timetables. The government, they said, was in the dubious position of holding people indefinitely without charging them with a crime.

"It's gotten to where we're really in uncharted waters," said Lee Gelernt, a senior lawyer for the Immigrants' Rights Project at the American Civil Liberties Union. "The government has effectively reversed the presumption of innocence. They are holding people for months once their immigration cases are concluded while they look to see if there is a reason to bring other charges."

Immigration lawyers say the new policy, created by Attorney General John Ashcroft shortly after Sept. 11, has led to a collision between the traditional rights afforded foreigners and the need for heightened security. Many of the detainees do not have lawyers, but some who do have begun to file lawsuits in federal court demanding their release.

In response, the Justice Department official said: "There is some justification in their position that we can't hold the detainees forever. But we feel we do have some leeway."

Law enforcement officials said that some detainees were still being scrutinized but that many others had been released recently or were simply awaiting completion of travel arrangements or new passport documents. More than 700 people were held on immigration charges after Sept. 11. Officials said on Friday that they were still holding 327 people, including the 87 already under departure orders.

Interviews with defense lawyers suggest that the clearance process has delayed the release of many of the detainees held in New York and New Jersey. A close look at some cases shows that the inquiries have created murky standoffs in which the F.B.I. cannot prove that the detainees are dangerous and the detainees cannot allay the F.B.I.'s suspicions.

For instance, Ahmed Alenany, a cabdriver in Brooklyn, was caught in the post–Sept. 11 dragnet when it was found that he had overstayed his visa. He said he told an immigration judge in October that he did not need a lawyer and just wanted to get home to his wife and two children in Cairo as soon as possible.

When the judge suggested that deportation would be the fastest route, he said, he agreed to be deported.

In a recent interview at the Middlesex County Jail in New Jersey, Mr. Alenany, 50, who was trained as a doctor, said he had divided his time between New York and Egypt in the last five years.

He said he came to New York seeking specialized medical training, but he had little money and ended up driving a cab. He was arrested on Sept. 21 after a police officer in Brooklyn questioned why he had stopped in a no-parking zone and found that his visa had expired.

It is not hard to see why investigators were suspicious. Mr. Alenany said he had taped a photograph of the White House in the back window of his cab. He had also fastened a picture of the World Trade Center to his glove box, with a piece of black tape slanting across an upper corner.

He said he told F.B.I. agents that he had lived for nine years in Saudi Arabia, where he also drove a cab before getting a job as a doctor. Mr. Alenany also volunteered that around 1990, he dropped off a disabled man at the home of a wealthy benefactor, who gave the passenger $50. He said he later heard that the benefactor was Osama bin Laden.

But in the interview in jail, Mr. Alenany said all these events were more innocent than they might have sounded to the F.B.I.

He said he placed the photographs in his cab to show his sympathy for America's suffering and the black mark across the top of the World Trade Center photograph was a common Egyptian symbol of mourning. He also said he had never seen or met Mr. bin Laden and was not even sure the house he went to as a cabdriver was Mr. bin Laden's.

"I told that story voluntarily, but I feel that I put myself in a very critical position," Mr. Alenany said, adding that he was in despair over losing his dream of living in America.

"When I was 6 years of age, I was starving," he said. "And I smelled a beautiful smell. And when I asked what it was, someone said it was cheese from America, a far, faraway land. From this time on I felt love for America."

But, he added: "Now I'm in very bad shape, sir. Sometimes I feel it's hopeless, that I will stay in this jail all my life."

Mr. Alenany said that law enforcement officials took him into custody on Sept. 21 and searched his $300-a-month room in Brooklyn the next day. He received his deportation order at a court hearing on Oct. 16. That means today is his 151st day in custody and the 125th since the deportation order.

After his room was searched, Mr. Alenany said, he did not hear from the F.B.I. again until Jan. 17, when agents visited him in jail. He said they told him that American intelligence agencies had information about, or had intercepted, a phone call in which he made anti-American comments. He said they did not say what he had said or tell him when the conversation had taken place. He said he denied making such statements.

In one other meeting, on Jan. 29, investigators sought his help, Mr. Alenany said. They asked him about immigration violations, unrelated to terrorism, involving other people he knew, he said.

Justice Department and immigration officials declined to comment on Mr. Alenany's case. But defense lawyers said that the effort to gather investigative leads could further delay the release of some detainees.

Mahmoud Allam, Egypt's consul general in New York, said his government had tried to help Mr. Alenany and other detained Egyptians.

"This is a common case—people who get decisions for deportation from a court, and then they are not implemented," Mr. Allam said. Egyptian officials endorsed efforts by the United States to tighten security, he said, but, referring to the difficulty of some detainees in getting out of jail, he added, "It reminds you of the famous Kafka story of 'The Trial.'"

Bhanu Goldsmith, a New Jersey lawyer, said she represented a detainee from Mauritania who agreed to leave in early November, prompting an immigration service lawyer to predict that the man would be home by Thanksgiving. But, Ms. Goldsmith said, she recently heard that the man was still in jail, awaiting F.B.I. clearance.

Officials at the immigration agency, which is part of the Justice Department, said they were ordered to move more slowly with those detained after Sept. 11 than with other visa violators.

Referring to the F.B.I. reviews, Andrea Quarantilla, the immigration service's district director in Newark, said, "There is certainly an extra step in the process."

Lawyers for the detainees say visa violators who agree to leave usually must leave in 60 days but can sometimes take as many as 120 days.

Federal law provides that deportations should take place within 90 days of a deportation order. But the Supreme Court has ruled that the immigration service can extend that to 180 days if other countries refuse to accept a deportee.

Civil rights lawyers said deportation laws were enacted to deal with cases in which the government was trying to make people leave. "But now we have the opposite situation, where the alien is ready to comply and leave but the government doesn't want to let him go," said Bryan Lonegan, a lawyer at the Legal Aid Society in New York.

The only recourse for detainees held longer, lawyers say, is to file writs of mandamus in the federal courts to try to force the immigration service to send them home, or to file writs of habeas corpus to seek release.

Aslan Soobzokov, a lawyer in Paterson, N.J., said he recently filed habeas corpus petitions for three people detained after Sept. 11 and the government quickly sent two of them back to their native country, Turkey.

Regis Fernandez, a lawyer in Newark, said that shortly after he filed a writ of mandamus on behalf of a 21-year-old Australian of Arab descent, the immigration service notified him on Friday that the man had suddenly been cleared to leave.

Justice Department officials said they recognized that such petitions could become the next battleground involving the detainees.

"I'm not saying that in this large universe of people we haven't made some mistakes and held some people longer than we wanted to," the senior Justice Department official said. But the F.B.I. was pushing to complete the background checks, he said, and had "no interest in detaining people who are not a threat to us."

7

At Risk of Prejudice: The Arab American Community (Teaching about Tragedy)

Zeina Azzam Seikaly

"If they find out that the attackers were Arab, will they put us in internment camps like the Japanese in World War II?" An Arab American boy posed this question to his parents in the wake of the terrorist attacks on September 11, 2001. His fears were not laid to rest in the week after the tragedy, when hundreds of hate crimes were perpetrated against Arab Americans, both Muslim and Christian. These included verbal and physical attacks, shootings, bomb and death threats, and vandalism against homes, businesses, and places of worship. A general mood of hostility toward Arabs and Muslims was evident among the American public. The communities found themselves bearing the blame for the tragedies that had unfolded at the World Trade Center and the Pentagon.

Media commentators, community leaders, politicians, and President Bush spoke out against the scapegoating and ill treatment of Arabs and Muslims. Likewise, school administrators and educators scrambled to find ways to stave off the discrimination and stereotyping that would eventually find their way to their students. After teaching tolerance and an appreciation for diversity for

"At Risk of Prejudice: The Arab American Community," by Zeina Azzam Seikaly from *Social Education* 65, No. 6 (October 2001): 349–351. Copyright © National Council for the Social Studies. Reprinted by permission.

many years, teachers, multicultural coordinators, and guidance counselors now wondered how to stop a tide of prejudice from seeping into their classrooms. How can we teach about the Arab world in an objective way?, they wondered. Where can we obtain appropriate resources about the Arab world and Islam? What can be done to allay the fears of Arab and Muslim students and provide them with a safe and nurturing environment?

THE ARAB WORLD AS THE "OTHER"

Teachers often say that before starting a unit on the Middle East, they have to spend time guiding students to "unlearn" the stereotypes that the media and popular culture have propagated for decades. The terrorist, the harem girl, the wealthy oil shaikh, and the "mysterious East" are but a few of the impressions that many Americans have about the Arab world—from cartoons and comic books to TV shows and feature-length movies. Such images serve to exoticize that area of the world and make it strange and unfamiliar and different. We know that lumping any ethnic or racial group—in this case, 250 million Arabs—into categories, especially hostile ones, provides fertile ground for discrimination and "othering." Arabs become the "other," a people and a culture that exist outside Americans' concepts of what is "good" and "civilized." Essentially, a person begins to feel that she or he has nothing to do with "that group."

The textbooks available to teachers deal more seriously with the Arab world but still have some common defects. First of all, they often present Arabs as a homogeneous people (in fact, there is much diversity in the Arab world) and use photographs that reinforce stereotypes, such as camels in a desert and nomadic peoples. (1) Although these do exist, such glimpses only show one aspect of life in Arab countries. Images of urbanization, industry, farming, the arts, strong family ties, education, and sea coasts and mountains all would add important breadth and understanding to our knowledge of Arab society.

Second, textbooks often focus on the Arab world as a "region of conflict" without properly exploring Arab culture, civilization, and history. The result of this treatment is to reinforce stereotypes of Arabs as a violent people. Of course, there is conflict in the Arab world, but the last hundred years have also witnessed conflicts of extraordinary magnitude in the world as a whole. When we teach about our own historical conflicts or those of other western countries, we give those conflicts a context by showing how they fitted into and affected our views of ourselves as a people, with our distinctive aspirations, values, and way of life. Teaching about conflicts involving Arabs without teaching about Arab culture and civilization can lead to a distorted, one-dimensional image of Arabs. Offering a fuller view of Arab history and culture would go a long way toward fostering a deeper appreciation of the Arab world, and it would encourage students to see that in many ways "Arabs are just like us." It is important that educators provide context to discussions that deal with the Arab world; for example, subjects like political Islam, Arab women's rights, sanctions against Iraq, or oil and economics must be studied and analyzed in the light of their full social, political, and historical background.

The starting point for all this is perhaps an improved understanding of history. In one view of history commonly held in the West, respect is given to the achievements of the ancient Greeks and Romans, but a dark period is then considered to have elapsed until the European Renaissance, which is treated as the start of modern history. In this view, ideas and scientific advances born in the Renaissance have traveled eastward and awakened other peoples, including the Arabs. Historians of the medieval era know otherwise. Arab/Islamic civilization flourished in the era preceding the Renaissance; it was Arabs who translated ancient Greek works, and then expanded and elaborated on them, thus helping to lay the groundwork for the Renaissance. Arabic-language treatises on such subjects as astronomy, mathematics, optics, chemistry, philosophy, and religion abounded and helped bridge the gap between the wisdom of the ancient world and that of the modern one.

Partly because of the emphasis on conflict in the region, the Arab-Israeli conflict often is the focus of a unit of study on the Middle East. This seemingly intractable dilemma poses difficult challenges for teachers, and some have told me that they opt not to teach it at all. "American policy as it relates to the Middle East is not usually covered in the classroom," one teacher notes, adding, "That's a hornet's nest that most teachers prefer not to tackle." To be sure, many common myths are associated with this conflict as well, the prevalent one being that the Palestinians are terrorists bent on destroying Israel. When teaching about this conflict, it is important to humanize the Palestinian people and include the study of their history, culture, life under occupation, and national aspirations. A lasting peace can only result from a just settlement that recognizes the rights of both Israelis and Palestinians.

WHO ARE THE ARAB AMERICANS?

There are approximately three million Americans of Arab descent, the majority of whom trace their roots to five national groups: Lebanese, Syrians, Palestinians, Egyptians, and Iraqis. The early Arab immigrants started to travel to the United States in the late nineteenth and early twentieth centuries, most of them from the area that is present-day Lebanon and Syria. The population of Arab Americans spans all fifty states, with large concentrations in three major metropolitan areas: Los Angeles and southern California, Detroit and Dearborn in southeastern Michigan, and the New York/New Jersey area.

A sizeable percentage of the community is Christian (all denominations, including Maronite, Melkite, Chaldean, Eastern Orthodox, and Coptic), owing to the high numbers of Christian immigrants from Greater Syria (an area ruled by the Ottoman Empire) prior to World War I. The number of Arab Muslims—both Sunni and Shi'a—increased as immigrants from all Arab countries settled in the United States, largely in the second half of the twentieth century. They, along with South Asian, East Asian, African, African American, and American Muslims, bring the number of Muslims in the United States to approximately seven million.

Arab Americans have played an important role in American society in all areas—the arts and literature, government and politics, business, medicine, sports, and the entertainment industry. Notable examples are poet and writer Kahlil Gibran, consumer advocate and presidential candidate Ralph Nader, heart surgeon Michael DeBakey, actor Danny Thomas, former Health and Human Services Secretary Donna Shalala, former Senator James Abourezk, U.S. Energy Secretary Spencer Abraham, football star Doug Flutie, children's author and poet Naomi Shihab Nye, and disk jockey Casey Kasem. Like other naturalized ethnic groups, Arab Americans have served in the U.S. military in World Wars I and II and the Korean and Vietnam Wars, and continue to serve their country today.

Arab Americans have organized in political, civic, social, and religious organizations, though they are generally not an insular community and participate actively in American life. More than 80 percent of the community's members are U.S. citizens and identify themselves as Democrats, Republicans, or independents.

As a result of the Arab-Israeli conflict and the United States' strong support of Israel, a politically charged atmosphere surrounds Arab Americans. Within the Arab American community, a strong perception exists that there is a bias toward Israel in American foreign policy and that the United States is not an impartial mediator in the conflict. Arab Americans also face the ramifications of political Islam as it plays out on the world scene, and the negative public opinions that it generates in the United States. One of the community's concerns is the current application of anti-terrorism laws, which some believe unfairly target Arab Americans and sanction the use of secret evidence against them, thereby jeopardizing their right to due process under the law. The U.S. Attorney General's office would like to expand its powers to use phone and computer tapping and other methods of intelligence collection. These moves concern many legal professionals in that they might erode Arab Americans' civil liberties and constitutional rights.

ARAB AMERICAN STUDENTS

The horrific events of September 11 catapulted the "Arab terrorist" stereotype to the forefront of America's consciousness. Because many of the terrorists were found to be Arab, all Arabs became suspect, and Arab Americans were on the receiving end of the American public's anger. To be sure, many religious and civic organizations offered support and solidarity to the community; such sentiments were evident at numerous inter-faith services and speeches of political leaders.

Arab American students, however, have been feeling afraid, unsafe, and insecure. Their peers have taunted them about their nationality or blamed them indirectly for the terrorist acts. "My father says you are bad people," one child told an Arab American peer, according to an elementary school guidance counselor. The parents are experiencing worse, threats such as phone calls or letters saying, "Go home. We don't want you in our country."

Arab American and Muslim students need to feel protected and safe in school. Guidance counselors must be alerted when such incidents occur, and teachers need to show support and understanding. It is not helpful to act in a dismissive manner and to say that the problem will go away. Teenagers, in particular, can experience great anxiety if rejected by their classmates, and feelings of abandonment and depression may set in. Some students might begin to question their self-worth, and their self-esteem may diminish. Still others might feel angry and act out, and they will need counseling.

Teachers and school administrators have a responsibility to protect these students and assure them that they are safe from verbal, physical, and psychological harm. Educators need to help all students understand that the actions of a few do not reflect on an entire population, just as the actions of Timothy McVeigh, the Oklahoma City bomber, do not mirror all Americans. Most Arabs and Muslims, like most Americans, are law-abiding citizens who work and have families and want nothing more than to live peaceful and fulfilling lives.

Students might want to know that many Muslims and Arab Americans died in the World Trade Center tragedy, and that their families are grieving for them and searching for answers as well. Arab Americans—both Muslim and Christian—are actively involved in the rescue operations, donating blood, organizing fund drives for the victims, and holding special religious services and vigils.

Zeina Azzam Seikaly is Outreach Coordinator at the Center for Contemporary Arab Studies, Georgetown University, Washington, D.C.

RESOURCES ON ARABS AND ARAB AMERICANS

Books

- Ashabranner, Brent. An Ancient Heritage: The Arab American Minority. New York: HarperCollins, 1991.
- Bushnaq, Inea. Arab Folktales. New York: Pantheon Books, 1986.

- Hayes, John R., ed. The Genius of Arab Civilization: Source of Renaissance. Cambridge, Mass.: The MIT Press, 1983, 2nd edition.

- Hourani, Albert. A History of the Arab Peoples. New York: Warner Books, 1991, and Cambridge, Mass.: Belknap Press of Harvard University Press, 1991.

- Naff, Alixa. The Arab Americans. New York: Chelsea House Publishers, 1988.

- Nye, Naomi Shihab. The Space Between Our Footsteps: Poems and Paintings from the Middle East. New York: Simon and Schuster, 1998.

- Pearson, Robert P. Through Middle Eastern Eyes (accompanied by a Teaching Strategies booklet). New York: A CITE Book, 1993.

- Samhan, Helen. "Arab Americans." Grolier's Multimedia Encyclopedia; www.grolier.com.

- Shabbas, Audrey, ed. The Arab World Studies Notebook. Berkeley, Calif.: AWAIR (Arab World and Islamic Resources) and Washington D.C.: Middle East Policy Council, 1998.

- Shaheen, Jack G. Arab and Muslim Stereotyping in American Popular Culture. Washington, D.C.: Center for Muslim-Christian Understanding, Georgetown University, 1997.

- Tamari, Steve. Who Are the Arabs? Washington, D.C.: Center for Contemporary Arab Studies, Georgetown University, 1999.

- Zogby, John. Arab America Today: A Demographic Profile of Arab Americans. Washington, D.C.: Arab American Institute, 1990.

Videos

- Hart, Robbie and Luc Cote. Turning 16: Part 4: The Story of Eman. Oley, PA: Bullfrog Films, 1994. 30 minutes. A documentary detailing the life of a sixteen-year-old Egyptian girl; her dreams, expectations, and responsibilities are explored within an Arab-Muslim cultural context. Part of a larger series detailing teenagers of different cultures.

- Mandell, Joan. Tales from Arab Detroit. Detroit, MI: Olive Branch Productions, 1995. 45 minutes. A documentary following the visit of traditional Egyptian musicians to an Arab American community in Michigan. Explores the identity issues arising from mixed cultural backgrounds, and portrays the Arab American community through the lenses of several generations. Offers an overview of the diversity found within an Arab American community. Appropriate for grades 6–12.

- Young Voices from the Arab World: The Lives and Times of Five Teenagers. Washington, D.C.: Amideast, 1998. 30 minutes. A collage-style documentary of the lives of five young Arabs living in Jordan, Lebanon, Egypt, Kuwait, and Morocco. Narrated by Casey Kasem. Appropriate for grades 4–9.

Internet Resources

- American Arab Anti-Discrimination Committee: www.adc.org

- Amideast: www.amideast.org

- Arab American Institute: www.aaiusa.org

- Arab World and Islamic Resources (AWAIR): www.telegraphave.com/gui/awairproductinfo.html

- Center for Contemporary Arab Studies, Georgetown University: www.ccasonline.org

- Council on Islamic Education: www.cie.org

- Middle East and Islamic World Film Collections: www.lib.unc.edu/cdd/crs/foreign/meiw/films.html

- Middle East Network Information Center: link.lanic.utexas.edu/menic
- National Council on U.S.-Arab Relations/High School Model Arab League: www.ncusar.org/modelarableague/aboutmal.html
- Network of Educators on the Americas/Teaching for Social and Economic Justice: www.teachingforchange.org

NOTE

1. One common public misconception of Arabs that textbooks should always correct is that all Arabs are Muslim. The Arab world contains significant Christian minorities in such countries as Egypt, Lebanon, Syria, and the Palestinian territories.

Hispanic Immigration

8

Two Americas?
A Massive Wave of
Hispanic Immigration Is
Raising Questions about
Identity and Integration

Joseph Contreras, with Jennifer Ordonez in Los Angeles
and Arian Campo-Flores in Miami

In his provocative 1996 book "The Clash of Civilizations," Samuel P. Huntington argued that culture would replace ideology as the principal cause of conflict in the 21st century. The Harvard professor foresaw a collision of "Western arrogance, Islamic intolerance and [Chinese] assertiveness" that would dominate global politics in the post–cold-war era. In his new book, "Who Are We? The Challenges to America's National Identity," the conservative Cassandra looks at American society through that same cultural prism and discerns an internal clash of civilizations: the new war is between the country's white majority and its burgeoning Hispanic population.

"The most serious challenge to America's traditional identity comes from the immense and continuing immigration from Latin America, especially from

"Two Americas? A massive wave fo Hispanic immigration is raising questions about identity and integration," by Joseph Contreras from *Newsweek*, March 22, 2004. Reprinted by permission.

Mexico," writes Huntington in an excerpt from the forthcoming book published in Foreign Policy magazine. "As their numbers increase, Mexican Americans feel increasingly comfortable with their own culture and often contemptuous of American culture." Never one to shrink from controversy, the 76-year-old academic asks pointedly: "Will the United States remain a country with a single national language and a core Anglo-Protestant culture? By ignoring this question, Americans acquiesce to their eventual transformation into two peoples with two cultures (Anglo and Hispanic) and two languages (English and Spanish)."

The backlash has not been long in coming—from both sides of the Rio Grande. The Mexican author Carlos Fuentes labeled Huntington a "racist" in the influential Mexico City newspaper Reforma last week and deplored the professor's "stigmatizing of the Spanish language as a practically subversive factor of division." The self-described conservative U.S. columnist David Brooks took issue with Huntington's Kulturkampf scenario in The New York Times. "The mentality that binds us is not well described by the words 'Anglo' or 'Protestant,'" wrote Brooks. "There are no significant differences between Mexican-American lifestyles and other American lifestyles."

At a time when white U.S. politicians are tripping over each other in hot pursuit of the Latino voter, Huntington's Hispanophobia has reopened some unresolved questions about identity and integration. Are Hispanics rejecting the powerful forces of American cultural assimilation, which swallowed up the successive waves of European immigrants who preceded them? Are their swelling ranks and enduring loyalty to Latin American culture and the Spanish language carving out Hispanic-dominated enclaves like Miami where, as Huntington puts it, native Anglos and African-Americans become "outside minorities that [can] often be ignored"? Or are Hispanics simply redefining the meaning of mainstream in an ever more diverse, multicultural United States of America?

Statistics amply document the rise of the Hispanic American. Native and foreign-born U.S. residents of Latin American ancestry overtook blacks as the largest American minority three years ago and are fast approaching the 40 million mark. Between 8 million and 10 million of these Hispanics are thought to be illegal immigrants, and nearly 70 percent are Mexicans. If current birthrates and rising levels of immigration continue, Hispanics could attain majority status in California by 2018, and may account for fully one quarter of all Americans by the middle of this century.

It is the roughly 22 million Mexicans in America who most trouble Huntington. He contrasts the success story of Miami's Cuban-Americans—who transformed that city into the economic capital of Latin America—with the Mexican immigrants of the American Southwest, the overwhelming percentage of whom are described as "poor, unskilled and poorly educated." The children of this Mexican underclass, concludes Huntington, "are likely to face similar conditions."

Mexican-Americans and other Hispanics are not quite the insular tail of American society that Huntington contends. They are moving up the socio-economic ladder—albeit more slowly than the white ethnic groups who preceded them. Historically speaking, it's important to remember that this wave of immigration is still relatively young. In the case of Mexican immigration, it soared after 1965: 2.2 million Mexicans legally moved to the United States in the 1990s, up sharply from the 640,000 who lawfully immigrated to El Norte in the 1970s, and these figures don't encompass the possibly larger numbers who entered the country illegally.

More Latinos are going to college—the rate has risen from 16 percent in 1980 to 22 percent in 2000—and they're making more money: their median household income rose by 4.3 percent between 1988 and 1999. The Washington-based Pew Hispanic Center reports that teenage and young-adult Latinos work and earn more than anyone else in their age group, whites included. Admittedly, one reason is that many do not go to college, and the center found high unemployment rates among second-generation Hispanic youths. But beyond the age of 25, second-generation Latinos with college degrees earn more on average than white workers with comparable educational backgrounds.

Rocky Chavez spent many childhood summers picking grapes in California's San Joaquin Valley alongside his Mexican-American aunts and uncles. The Los Angeles native recalls telling his U.S.-born father, one of 18 children, how much he disliked the backbreaking menial labor. "Then get an education," his father responded. Rocky did, earning a college degree. Today the 52-year-old retired Marine colonel speaks little Spanish; he is the principal of a new charter high school in the town of Oceanside, California, and wants to run for mayor as a Republican. "When my father moved us to Torrance he pulled us away from the Latino community," says Chavez, the proud father of three college-educated children. "I assimilated, and I tell my kids, 'You know, we went from a migrant family to a family with a son who just graduated from the best medical school in the nation'."

Hispanics have become accepted in one important respect—as consumers. Their enormous buying power has opened the eyes of big business, especially in an era when Latino celebrities like J. Lo and Ricky Martin vie for top billing with Britney Spears and Brad Pitt. Anna Brockway, the brand-marketing director at jeans maker Levi Strauss, says she doesn't think in terms of Hispanic culture versus mainstream U.S. culture anymore. An English-language ad for Levi's that aired during the January 2002 Super Bowl featured a young Latino model strutting along the grimy streets of Mexico City. Some of Brockman's colleagues asked her why the company picked a "Hispanic ad" for the broadcast. "Hispanic culture is American culture at this point," she explained.

That's especially true among young people. Latinos account for the highest percentage of youths under the age of 18 in seven of the 10 largest U.S. cities. Their numbers will continue to swell for the foreseeable future: the Latino teen population is projected to grow by 36 percent over the next 16 years, while their white peers will decline by 3 percent, according to California-based Hispanic marketing expert Isabel Valdes.

There is disagreement about the degree to which these youngsters and their parents are learning and speaking English. A recent study by the U.S. Association of Hispanic Advertising Agencies (AHAA) found that 68 percent of Latinos between the ages of 18 and 34 are either bilingual or identify Spanish as their language of choice. But other research has turned up very different results pointing in the direction of assimilation. A nationwide 2002 survey by the Pew Hispanic Center and the Kaiser Family Foundation found that among adult Latinos whose parents were immigrants, only 7 percent relied on Spanish as their primary language. Nearly half had no Spanish skills at all, and the rest were bilingual. The corresponding figures were even lower for the U.S.-born children of those second-generation Hispanic adults: less than a quarter were bilingual, and the number of those Latinos who spoke only Spanish was not statistically significant. "The transition from Spanish to English is virtually complete in one generation," says Pew Hispanic Center director Roberto Suro. "Hispanics are undergoing a powerful process of change no less than anyone else who has come to these shores."

Lest he be accused of being a xenophobic bigot, Huntington concedes that biculturalism is not in itself a bad thing. But he is troubled by the concept of bilingual education and by the idea that Americans may need to learn Spanish to communicate with their fellow citizens. In fact, the United States already is a profoundly bilingual society throughout the Southwest and Texas, in most of California, and in cities from Chicago and New York to Miami. The days when one country meant one language, one culture and apparently one Protestant faith are long gone—if they ever existed in the first place. Millions of Hispanics are assimilating, but they are also putting their own distinctive stamp on what assimilation will signify for future generations. And that is not the result of some apocalyptic showdown between two antithetical civilizations.

Whose values? Hispanics could attain majority status in California by 2018 (text/graph) Hispanic America: A Nation Within a Nation: As immigration—legal and otherwise—from Latin America soars, the arrivals are joining Spanish speaking citizens to challenge old ideas of what being 'American' means. (graphic omitted)

9

The Plight of Immigrants from Mexico

Edward P. Lazear

Immigrants from Mexico do far worse when they migrate to the United States than do immigrants from other countries. Those difficulties are more a reflection of U.S. immigration policy than they are of underlying cultural differences. The following facts from the 2000 U.S. Census reveal that Mexican immigrants do not move into mainstream American society as rapidly as do other immigrants.

1. Eighty percent of non–Mexican immigrants are fluent in English. Among Mexicans, the number is 49 percent.

2. Non–Mexican (working) immigrants have an average wage income of $21,000 a year. Mexican immigrants have an average wage income of $12,000 a year.

3. The typical non–Mexican immigrant has a high school diploma. The typical Mexican immigrant has less than an eighth-grade education.

4. Compared to other Hispanics, only 49 percent of Mexican immigrants are fluent in English, compared to 62 percent of non–Mexican Hispanics.

5. Mexican average incomes are about 75 percent that of other Hispanic immigrants, and Mexican immigrants have about two and a half fewer years of schooling.

Two other facts are worth noting. First, Mexican immigrants live in communities where 15 percent of the residents were also born in Mexico. Non-Mexican immigrants live in communities where fewer than 3 percent of the residents are from their native land. Second, Mexican immigrants account

"The plight of immigrants from Mexico," by Edward Lazear as appeared in *National Review,* December 13, 2004. Reprinted by permission of Edward Lazear.

for a much higher proportion of the immigrant population than does any other group—29 percent in the 2000 census.

The last two points are key. Individuals become assimilated when their incentives to do so are great. An immigrant from Mexico who moves to East Los Angeles can survive knowing only Spanish and interacting primarily with people from her or his own community. A Bulgarian immigrant to Billings, Montana, must learn English quickly or return to Bulgaria.

A number of studies suggest that the most important factor in explaining English fluency and other aspects of assimilation is the proportion of individuals in one's community who come from his or her native land. When there are many, assimilation is slow; when there are few, assimilation is rapid. Mexicans often do poorly because they have been part of a large wave of immigrants who have similar cultures, languages, and backgrounds.

One other factor is that U.S. immigration policy selects immigrants from Mexico primarily on the basis of family connection rather than skill. Immigrants from other countries are more likely to enter and take jobs in highly skilled occupations. In fact, our most able immigrants come from North Africa— Morocco, Algeria, and Libya. Is this because those countries have the world's best educational systems and cultures? No, it is because it is virtually impossible to enter the United States from those countries. The only North Africans to get in are highly educated and talented.

Nothing inherent in Mexicans causes difficulties for them when they come to the United States. Instead, it is our immigration policy that encourages the formation of large, insular Mexican communities. Additionally, our policies do not employ the same selection criteria for Mexicans as they do for applicants from other countries.

Moving in the direction of skills-based immigration and away from relative-based immigration is one step we can take to ensure that immigrants do well and become integrated when they come to the United States. Moreover, a conscious policy that encourages a more balanced distribution of countries from which we draw immigrants will improve the speed of assimilation and raise the incomes of both immigrants and U.S. natives.

Edward P. Lazear *is the Morris Arnold Cox Senior Fellow at the Hoover Institution and the Jack Steele Parker Professor of Human Resources, Management and Economics at Stanford University's Graduate School of Business.*

10

Police Hope to Connect with Hispanics: Citizens Police Academy Offers Chance to Experience Officers' World

Kenneth A. Gailliard

Dec. 29—Hundreds of Myrtle Beach area residents have reported gaining better understanding of local law enforcement after attending the Myrtle Beach Police Department's Citizens Police Academy, but police want more individuals from the area's growing Hispanic communities to participate.

The academy has helped more than 200 residents get to know police officers and understand their work since it started in 2000, said Lt. Tommy Chestnut, who oversees the program. Jack and Sandy Cheape of Murrells Inlet say their experience in the academy was "eye opening."

"We got to see up close what police have to go through and how they interact with people," Sandy Cheape said. "More people should do it." Myrtle Beach Police Chief Warren Gall said the police department is trying to get more Hispanic residents to apply for the program.

An attempt earlier this year to hold a one-day seminar for Hispanic residents did not get good response, Gall said. At least one Hispanic applicant is being considered for the spring Citizens Police Academy session that begins Jan. 9, Gall said. "It would be a plus to have people in the [Hispanic] community who are close to the police," said Min Alexander, a founding member of the Myrtle Beach group Latinoamericanos en Accion and an active member in the Puerto Rican social club Coneccion Boricua. "People often don't know who to go to ask questions, and there are a lot of battered women who don't know how to get help."

Other police agencies across the country that offer citizens academies also are using the training to reach their Hispanic populations. One of those is the Arlington County Police Department in Virginia. Arlington police completed a session targeted for Hispanics earlier this year, said Sgt. David Reiten of the Arlington County Police Department.

"It was the first class solely in Spanish, and we used translation technology," Reiten said. "We have had lots of interest." He said arrangements already are being made for the next Spanish session.

Reiten said his department's effort "vastly improved communication between the police and the Hispanic community." Myrtle Beach police do not have the resources to hold a Spanish-only 10-week session, Gall said, but "we may look at an abbreviated Spanish-speaking class using a Spanish-speaking officer and walk before we run." He said increasing the Hispanic participation in the academies would help create links between the department and those residents. "It helps humanize officers in the eyes of the citizens, and they build and develop relationships," he said. "In the Hispanic community, it would help to have them trust us and know who we are. They have to be able to see us as an agency there to help." The Myrtle Beach Citizens Police Academy covers topics such as crime-scene investigation, criminal domestic violence, gun safety and firearms simulation. Participants also are allowed to ride along with police, Cheape said. "Riding with them made me realize they are always watching and they can see things we can't see," Cheape said. "I watched them handle domestic situations, and they were very diplomatic. I think people would have an incredible amount of respect for the way they handle situations." She said her experience turned her into an ambassador for the police department.

Although it is not the intent of the program, Chestnut said several former participants have returned to offer voluntary assistance to the department, and some have gone on to become police officers.

All academy applicants must qualify and be approved to participate.

Local authorities don't want to be perceived as immigration police, Gall said, but individuals must be U.S. citizens to participate.

"We are seeing a separation between the Hispanic community and law enforcement," Gall said. "We want to be proactive. When we need their help in helping them; we find it hard to get cooperation because of a lack of trust." Contact KENNETH A. GAILLIARD at 626-0312 or kgailliard@thesunnews .com [mailto:kgailliard@thesunnews.com]. Applications for the Citizens Police

Academy are available at the Myrtle Beach Police Department on Oak Street at Mr. Joe White Avenue, or at the police department annex on the former Myrtle Beach Air Force Base. Requirements:

At least 21 years old. Must live or work within the Horry County (first preference is given to residents of Myrtle Beach). Complete a personal history form. Background investigation, including criminal-history check. Must ride with officers a minimum of 25 hours (five hours on day shift, five hours on evenings, five hours on midnights, five hours with Special Operations or Beach Patrol and five hours observing dispatch/police service desk). If the student participates in the optional Saturday class, the number of hours drops to 20 hours, four on each shift. Attend at least eight of the 10 meetings of the Citizens Police Academy. Applicants are selected by the chief of police through the application process. Contact Sgt. Tommy Chestnut at 918-1803 or e-mail him at tchestnut@cityofmyrtlebeach.com [mailto:tchestnut@cityofmyrtlebeach.com].

Distributed by Knight Ridder/Tribune Business News.

11

President Proposes Creation of Department of Homeland Security— INS Functions to Be Transferred (Legal Report)

Francesco Isgro

President Bush's announcement on June 6, 2002, to create a permanent Cabinet-level Department of Homeland Security, has catapulted the future of the beleaguered Immigration and Naturalization Service (INS) into a higher orbit of uncertainty. The historic proposal, delivered to Congress on June 18, 2002, would merge a dozen agencies, among them the INS, into the new department. In announcing the plan, the President vowed that this great country will lead the world to safety, security, peace and freedom. Bush explained that the reason for creating the new department was not to increase the size of government, "but to increase its focus and effectiveness."

The President's proposal came at the heels of passage by the House of Representatives of the Barbara Jordan Immigration Reform and Accountability Act of 2002. That bill, which passed the House by an overwhelming margin of 405-9, would restructure the INS by creating two separate agencies. The Senate, too, has legislation pending to revamp the INS.

Proposals to restructure the INS have been floating throughout Washington for many years without success. However, in the post–September 11 climate, the passage of legislation by this Congress to restructure the INS was almost assured. Now, in light of the President's proposal and the current political tones in Washington, it appears that the starting point for any restructuring of the INS would have to be within the framework of the new department. Therefore, legislative plans still on the table would most likely have to fit within the scheme of the proposed department.

THE DEPARTMENT OF
HOMELAND DEFENSE

As we recently observed in Migration World, "immigration enforcement has become a principal component of the war against terrorism." Thus, it is not surprising that the President's proposal would transfer the functions of the INS to the Department of Homeland Defense.

The proposal would merge dozens of agencies, including the INS, creating a staff of more than 160,000 workers in the new department. Under the President's proposal, the Department of Homeland Security would be organized into four divisions: Border and Transportation Security; Emergency Preparedness and Response; Chemical, Biological, Radiological, and Nuclear Countermeasures; and Information Analysis and Infrastructure Protection.

The new department would be charged with securing our nation's air, land, and sea borders. The INS functions would be transferred to the Division for Border and Transportation Security. According to an organizational chart proposed by the White House, this division would further be divided into Border Security, Transportation Security, Coast Guard, and Immigration Services. The Border Security section would combine the U.S. Border Patrol, Customs, and other agencies involved in border controls. The Immigration and Visa Services would include the INS, minus the Border Patrol, and would be further separated into immigration services and enforcement. According to the White House, the new department "would assume the legal authority to issue visas for foreign nationals and admit them into the country. The State Department would continue to administer the visa application and issuance process."

However, the bill submitted to Congress uses very broad language and does not include many specifics as to the division's actual organization. For example, Section 401 of the proposed bill would relegate responsibility for border and transportation security to the Under Secretary for Border and Transportation Security, whose responsibilities would include:

- preventing the entry of terrorists and the instruments of terrorism into the United States;
- securing the borders, territorial waters, ports, terminals, waterways, and air, land, and sea transportation systems of the United States, including managing and coordinating governmental activities at ports of entry;
- administering the immigration and naturalization laws of the United States, including the establishment of rules, in accordance with Section 403, governing the granting of visas or other forms of permission, including parole, to enter the United States to individuals who are not citizens or lawful permanent residents thereof; and
- administering the customs laws of the United States.

Specifics on the precise restructuring of the INS under the new department have yet to be determined. Clearly, as the President stated in his message to the nation, the reorganization would seek to end "duplication and overlap" within the Executive Branch. An example of the current duplication and overlap of functions, the White House notes in a 28-page summary of the proposal, occurs when a ship enters a U.S. port. In such a case, Customs, INS, the Coast Guard, the U.S. Department of Agriculture, and others have overlapping jurisdictions over pieces of the arriving ship. To illustrate what happens under the current system, the White House points to the following scenario:

> "If the Coast Guard stops a ship at sea for inspection and finds there are illegal immigrants on the ship, the Coast Guard relies on the INS to enforce U.S. immigration law and prevent their entry. If the Coast Guard finds potentially dangerous cargo, it relies on Customs to seize the dangerous cargo. Unfortunately, these organizations may not always share information with each other as rapidly as necessary. So, instead of arresting potential terrorists and seizing dangerous cargo at sea, our current structure can allow these terrorists to enter our ports and potentially sneak into our society. The system might also allow the dangerous cargo to actually enter our ports and threaten American lives."

Thus, one likely outcome of the Administration's proposal is that the border functions will be under one chain of command. This restructuring of the border agencies is consistent with other legislative proposals, including one currently pending in the Senate. Consequently, the United States Border Patrol would be separated from the INS. What remains of the INS, namely, interior enforcement and services, would also be split, most likely along the enforcement and service lines.

The proposal that may generate the most contention is the language in Section 403 of the proposed bill, namely the authority to issue visas. Currently, U.S. consular officers issue visas under the administrative direction of the Secretary of State. Under the new proposal, the Secretary of the Department of Homeland Security would have "exclusive authority, through the Secretary of State, to issue regulations with respect to, administer, and enforce the provisions of that Act and all other immigration and nationality laws relating to the functions of diplomatic and consular officers of the United States in connection with the granting or refusal of visas." The Secretary of State would still have the authority to refuse a visa to an alien if he "deems such refusal necessary or advisable in the interests of the United States." Thus, it would appear that at a minimum the Secretary of Homeland Defense would set the legal standards for the issuance of visas. However, the broad language of Section 403 suggests that the visa issuance function of the Department of State will no longer be only a tool of foreign policy, but will also fall within the purview of homeland security.

The proposal submitted to Congress does not identify the Executive Office for Immigration Review (EOIR) as an agency that would be merged into the proposed Department. As we wrote in the last issue of Migration World, EOIR is likewise undergoing a major reorganization. Nonetheless, if the new department will administer all the immigration laws, EOIR may be absorbed as well. Because EOIR, through the immigration judges and the Board of Immigration Appeals, exercises an adjudicatory function, efforts to move EOIR to the proposed department are likely to generate substantial criticism from immigrants' rights groups. Whether such a transfer is actually proposed by the administration remains to be seen.

THE BARBARA JORDAN BILL

Because the proposed Department of Homeland Security would separate the service and enforcement function of the INS, it is worth summarizing the Barbara Jordan Immigration Reform and Accountability Act of 2002, the bill passed by the House on April 25, 2002.

The House bill would eliminate the INS and separate its functions into two bureaus: the Bureau of Immigration Enforcement (BIE) and the Bureau of Citizenship and Immigration Service (BCIS). Section 3 of the bill would also create the Office of the Associate Attorney General for Immigration Affairs (AAGIA). Even though the President's proposal would take the INS out of the Department of Justice, and thus no longer under the chain of command of the Attorney General, the functions of the proposed AAGIA may be taken over by an Assistant Secretary of Homeland Security. Under the House proposal, the AAGIA would supervise the work of the two bureaus and coordinate the administration of national immigration policy. However, the day-to-day immigration operations would be run and managed independently within each immigration bureau. A number of offices would be placed in the AAGIA, including the General Counsel, the Chief Financial Officer, the

Director of Shared Services, the Office of Professional Responsibility, the Office of Children's Affairs, and a newly created Office of the Ombudsman.

Section 4 of the bill would establish the BCIS, to be headed by a Director who would report directly to the AACIA. All adjudications of nonimmigrant and immigrant visa petitions, naturalization petitions, asylum and refugee adjudications, service center adjudications, and all other immigration benefit adjudications would be transferred to the BCIS. The bill would create sectors headed by sector directors, located in appropriate geographic regions, and for field offices headed by field directors. Service centers would be headed by directors and would be subject to the general supervision of their respective sector directors. Section 5 of the bill would also create an Office of the Ombudsman within the BCIS.

Section 6 of the bill would create the BIE, also to be headed by a director who would report directly to the AAGIA. The Border Patrol program, the detention and deportation program, the intelligence program, the investigation program, and the inspection program would be transferred to the BIE. The bill also calls for the creation of BIE sectors, field offices, and Border Patrol sectors.

IMPACT OF PRESIDENT'S PROPOSAL

The President's far-reaching proposal to create the Department of Homeland Security and to merge the INS within the new department will undoubtedly transform all immigration issues into homeland security issues. This shift, precipitated by the September 11 events, has already occurred in Washington to some degree. It is fair to say that the proposed legislation reflects not only the President's view but also the mood of the nation. Many years ago, when immigration was a labor issue, the INS was placed within the Department of Labor. Subsequently, when immigration became an enforcement issue, it was transferred to the Department of Justice. And, it is likely, that before the end of this year, the INS will be transferred to the Department of Homeland Security.

The implications for people who enter this country either legally or illegally are enormous. If security is the principal concern of immigration, then how the INS conducts business today, namely the granting of immigration benefits, will have to change dramatically. Law enforcement background checks would have to be made not on a pro forma basis, as in the past, but as a function of national security goals. Backlogs of cases would not be eliminated simply because the lines are too long. Rather, longer waiting times for immigration benefits would be acceptable because of security concerns.

Of course, it is too early in the discussion to predict how the issues will play out politically in Washington. But, as we have observed before in Migration

World, the winds of immigration reform have swiftly changed direction. For the moment, the prevailing winds are solidly behind the President's proposal.

* Senior Legal Counsel, Office of Immigration Litigation, Civil Division, U.S. Department of Justice, Adjunct Professor, Georgetown University Lass Center 1990–2000, David Clarke School of Law, 2001–2002. The views expressed by the author are not necessarily the views of the Department of Justice. The information appearing in this article is generalized and should not be considered a substitute for professional legal advice in specific situations.

Search and Seizure

12

State of the Stop (Fourth Amendment Vehicle Search Cases)

Marcia Coyle

Washington—Marcus Thornton's case was not the most important Fourth Amendment car-search challenge in the U.S. Supreme Court in recent years. But his defeat last week was a piece in a puzzle whose complete picture will show there is little or no constitutional protection left for the privacy interests of those using automobiles, say many court scholars.

And although Thornton v. U.S., No. 03-5165, won't make the top 10 of all-time important Fourth Amendment cases, the decision revealed that even among justices who have restricted the amendment's reach, there are some who are increasingly unhappy with parts of the vehicle-search doctrine.

Concurring in the judgment in Thornton, Justice Antonin Scalia, joined by Justice Ruth Bader Ginsburg, wrote that the court's effort to apply its search-incident-to-arrest doctrine to this particular case "stretches it beyond its breaking point."

Even though the court has recognized for years a reduced expectation of privacy in the use of vehicles, Justice Potter Stewart once noted that the Fourth Amendment does not declare open season on automobiles, said criminal procedure scholar Tracey Macklin of Boston University School of Law.

"But this court has gotten as close as it can get to declaring open season without actually issuing licenses," added Macklin, who filed an amicus brief supporting Thornton on behalf of the National Association of Criminal Defense Lawyers and the American Civil Liberties Union.

Shashanka S. Upadye of Chicago's Lord, Bissell & Brook, who filed an amicus brief supporting neither party, agreed with Macklin, adding, "When you look at the cases in their entirety, over a 20- to 30-year period, you see drivers don't have any rights; people don't have any rights in their purses or suitcases, and police can search trunks. Customs can literally destroy your car, not find anything and say you can put it back together. After a while, you start wondering, 'What can I do in a car?'"

OUTSIDE THE CAR

The question in Thornton was more of an outside-of-your-car search issue. The court took the case to resolve conflicting lower court rulings on whether a bright-line rule announced by the justices in 1981 allowing police to search a car incident to an arrest applies when the person arrested has left the vehicle.

Three years ago, a Norfolk, Va., police officer became suspicious of Thornton, who was driving a Lincoln Town Car with tags licensed to a Chevy.

Thornton pulled into a parking lot, parked his car and left it as the officer drove in behind him. The officer parked, went after Thornton and asked for his license. When Thornton appeared nervous and rambling, the officer asked if he had any narcotics or weapons on him. Thornton said no. The officer asked for and received consent to frisk Thornton. He felt a bulge in a pocket which revealed bags of marijuana and crack cocaine.

The officer handcuffed and arrested Thornton and put him in the back seat of the patrol car. He then searched Thornton's car and found a handgun.

In New York v. Belton, 453 U.S. 454 (1981), the high court held that when a police officer makes a lawful custodial arrest of an automobile's occupant, the Fourth Amendment allows the officer to search the vehicle's passenger compartment as a contemporaneous incident of the arrest.

Belton itself extended a 1969 ruling to automobiles. In Chimel v. California, 395 U.S. 752, the justices articulated the search-incident-to-arrest exception to the warrant requirement in a case where the arrestee was in his home. The scope of these searches, said the court, was the person of the arrestee and the area immediately surrounding him.

The court stated two justifications for this exception: to protect the safety of the police officers and to preserve any evidence from destruction or concealment.

In the high court, Thornton's counsel, Frank Dunham, a federal public defender, argued that Belton is limited to situations where the officer initiated contact with an arrestee while the arrestee was still in the car. That position, he said, is consistent with the two reasons for a search incident to arrest. But the government argued that that would encourage suspects to jump out of cars before the police initiated contact or would encourage police to rush contact with suspects before they leave the car, creating a "potentially explosive dynamic."

Scalia noted that court cases involving the Thornton factual scenario are "legion." Some courts, he added, have upheld these searches even when the squad car carrying the handcuffed arrestee has already left the scene.

"If it was ever true that the passenger compartment is 'in fact generally, even if not inevitably,' within the arrestee's immediate control at the time of the search, it certainly is not true today," he wrote, quoting Belton.

Justice Sandra Day O'Connor, who concurred in part, agreed, writing that "lower court decisions seem now to treat the ability to search a vehicle incident to the arrest of a recent occupant as a police entitlement rather than as an exception justified by the twin rationales" of Chimel.

However, the 7-2 majority, led by Chief Justice William H. Rehnquist, said Belton's bright-line rule applies. Justices John Paul Stevens and David H. Souter dissented, with Stevens saying, "The only genuine justification for extending Belton to cover such circumstances is the interest in uncovering potentially valuable evidence. In my opinion, that goal must give way to the citizen's constitutionally protected interest in privacy when there is already in place a well-defined rule limiting the permissible scope of a search of an arrested pedestrian."

But Rehnquist wrote, "In all relevant aspects, the arrest of a suspect who is next to a vehicle presents identical concerns regarding officer safety and the destruction of evidence as the arrest of one who is inside the vehicle."

NOT-SO-BRIGHT LINE

The scope of a search incident to an arrest has been a problem for the Supreme Court since "the beginning of Fourth Amendment time," said Ronald Allen of Northwestern University School of Law, with the court vacillating back and forth over how much authority an officer has on the basis of the arrest.

"There is a larger issue floating over all of this, which is the simple rules versus all-of-the-circumstances kind of approach," he said. "What the court has pretty consistently done over the last 30 years is move away from discretionary calls for the officer on the street and move toward bright-line rules. That's what's going on in Thornton.

"They're searching for a bright-line rule to apply to the problem of the scope of search incident to arrest, and one problem has to be when you arrest somebody in or near a car," he added.

But bright lines in the law are hard to draw with really sharp edges, said Allen and others. The line that emerges isn't always sensitive to the underlying justifications that gave rise to the exception—here a warrantless search, they explained.

And that is what Scalia is really complaining about in Thornton, said Allen. The two justifications for search incident to arrest—police safety and preservation of evidence—generally are not present when the arrestee is handcuffed and secured in a squad car.

"We've had 30 to 40 years of going to bright-line rules, and one of consequences is it will be overinclusive or underinclusive," added Allen. "Thornton, for example, is not the end of the story. There's still the question of when a person is arrested in close enough proximity to a car that the search extends to the car. And what if he is arrested in his house and the car is in garage of the house?"

IMPACT ON RIGHTS

The importance of Thornton-Belton's impact on Fourth Amendment automobile rights is particularly stark when seen in combination with the high court's ruling in Atwater v. Lago Vista, 532 U.S. 318 (2001), according to some Fourth Amendment scholars.

In Atwater, the high court held that a warrantless custodial arrest for a misdemeanor punishable by a fine—here failure to wear seat belts—did not violate the Fourth Amendment.

"Atwater allows custodial arrest for any traffic violation, no matter how trivial," said criminal procedure scholar Donald Dripps of the University of Minnesota Law School.

"If that gets combined with Belton authority, since nobody can operate a car in full compliance with all traffic laws all of the time, it gives police the practical power to search a vehicle anyone is operating."

Boston University's Macklin agrees, explaining, "In those states like Texas, Iowa and one or two others, a lot of police officers arrest for traffic offenses and Thornton is a real boon. If a cop asks to search the car and a person says no, he can say, 'I'm going to arrest you,' and then he can search the car."

Thornton was one of three Fourth Amendment auto cases decided this term. The other two were Maryland v. Pringle, No. 02-809, and Illinois v. Lidster, No. 02-1060.

In Pringle, the court held it does not violate the Fourth Amendment for a police officer to arrest all occupants of a car where drugs and a roll of cash were found in the passenger compartment and the multiple occupants all denied ownership.

In Lidster, the high court upheld the constitutionality of a police roadblock with the primary purpose of investigating and seeking witnesses to a prior crime.

NEXT TERM

Next term in Illinois v. Caballes, No. 03-923, the justices will examine whether police must have "reasonable articulable suspicion" to conduct a canine sniff during a routine traffic stop.

Thomas Davies of the University of Tennessee College of Law, whose Fourth Amendment writings are often cited in high court opinions, said he believes there is nothing left of the amendment's protections in the automobile context.

Besides extending the scope of search incident to arrest, he said, there is also the automobile-search exception, which allows police to search a car if they have probable cause to believe there is evidence or contraband inside.

"There may be one situation where police still need a warrant," he suggested. In a 1971 case, the high court examined the search of a car parked in front of the house of a suspect in the murder of a young girl.

"The court in that case said they needed a warrant. It was a parked car that he hadn't been in recently," said Davies.

The whole notion that people have limited expectations of privacy in their automobiles is a "stretch" and should be re-examined, added Davies.

Lord Bissell's Upadye agreed, saying, "They use the lame argument that vehicles are pervasively regulated. Are you telling me a house is not? I understand the government has to do certain things, such as roadblocks. At the same time, you've got to think in today's age, more people are driving and more business is being conducted from cars. I would think drivers assume they have some privacy in their vehicles, in their corporate trade secrets or the reports in their briefcase."

13

Breaking the Pattern of Racial Profiling: When Law Enforcement Officers Make Discretionary Judgments Based on Race, Can Litigation Put an End to Stop-and-Search Violations?

David Rudovsky

On a summer evening in 1991, four young African-Americans were returning to Delaware from a church service in Philadelphia. Although the driver had committed no traffic violations, police officers stopped the car just south of the Philadelphia International Airport and ordered the driver and passengers out. The officers conducted an intrusive search of the car and its occupants using a narcotics-trained police dog and detained the group for almost an hour until convinced that they were not transporting drugs.

To justify the stop, the police issued a warning for obstruction of the car's windshield by a thin piece of string hanging from the rear-view mirror (which could not have been observed by the officers before the stop). When one of the car's occupants asked why they had been stopped, an officer answered with surprising candor, "Because you are young, black, and in a high drug-trafficking area driving a nice car." (1)

Virtually everyone agrees that it is impermissible to stop or search someone solely on the basis of race, but many law enforcement officials and courts continue to assert that race is a legitimate factor in making policing decisions—even without specific racial description of a suspect.

Litigation and government investigations concerning allegations of racial profiling on the New Jersey Turnpike provide data demonstrating a long-standing pattern of profiling. In criminal cases arising from drug arrests, a court found substantial evidence that stops and searches were highly disproportionate based on race. (2) The court determined that blacks and whites violated traffic laws at about the same rate, but that 42 percent of stops and 73 percent of arrests were of African-American motorists. A study by New Jersey's attorney general found that searches of cars on the turnpike were even more racially disparate than the initial stops: 77 percent of all searches consented to were of minorities. (3)

A New York attorney general study of 175,000 pedestrian stops in New York City found a highly disproportionate number of minorities stopped. (4) It determined that African-Americans were stopped six times more frequently than whites; that in precincts where African-Americans constituted 10 percent or less of a largely white population, they were stopped 30 percent of the time; and that, adjusting for crime rates by race, African-Americans were stopped twice as often as whites.

RATIONALES FOR RACIAL PROFILING

Police defend their racially disparate practices by saying that generally, minorities commit more crimes than whites. They also hold that enforcement of criminal laws that are violated by whites and minorities in roughly even numbers (for example, narcotics violations) is disproportionate because the location and social impact of the same types of crimes justifies a more aggressive response in minority communities. They argue that current practices work.

Aggressive policing and targeting of minority communities have led to significant seizures of contraband, weapons, and fugitives—and a reduction in crime.

In the wake of September 11 events, advocates of racial and ethnic profiling point to the need for heightened suspicion regarding the activities of young Arabic men. The arrests and detention of hundreds of people after the terrorist attacks has created considerable controversy—many of these people would not have been subject to this treatment were it not for ethnic characteristics, and the government has not yet provided evidence linking them to terrorist activities. Furthermore, it is not likely that ethnic profiling will be any more useful or constitutional than racial profiling.

In the area in which racial profiling has been most controversial—narcotics enforcement—proponents' arguments do not withstand empirical and legal scrutiny. For example, the data do not indicate a minority-dominated drug trade. National drug abuse studies show that minorities possess and use drugs only slightly more frequently than whites do. (5) "The typical cocaine user is white, male, a high school graduate employed full time, and living in a small metropolitan area or suburb," former drug czar William Bennett has said. (6)

Arrest statistics are also misleading. New Jersey's attorney general pointed out that these statistics are "a self-fulfilling prophecy where law enforcement agencies rely on arrest data that they themselves generated as a result of the discretionary allocation of resources and targeted drug enforcement efforts." (7)

Empirical evidence from reviews of car stops and searches supports this view. On the New Jersey Turnpike, 10.5 percent of contraband seized during traffic stops came from white drivers and 13.5 percent from African-American drivers. (8) In Maryland, searches on I-95 resulted in "find rates" that were roughly equal by race. (9) In both states, mostly small amounts of drugs were seized, indicating possession for personal use.

Millions of drivers use these highways each day, yet so few stops or searches of motorists—black or white—result in contraband seizures that it's hard to justify stopping large numbers of African-Americans so the police can make the occasional seizure.

The logic behind racial profiling is faulty, as Ira Glasser, former executive director of the Americal Civil Liberties Union, has said:

> Even if most of the drug dealers in the Northeast corridor or in any particular neighborhood or city are black or Latino, it does not follow that most blacks and Latinos are drug dealers. . . . Think about it for a minute. Most players in the NBA are black. But if you were trying to get a team together, you wouldn't go out in the street and round up random African-Americans.
>
> It's a very simple, logical fallacy. The fact that most drug dealers are X does not mean that most X are drug dealers. (10)

In policing, as in many areas of contemporary American life, race matters—and it matters a lot. The substantial racial disparities documented in stop, frisk, and search practices cannot be fully explained or rationalized by crime patterns, police deployment, or policing tactics.

AUTOMOBILE STOPS

A series of U.S. Supreme Court decisions over the past 30 years has delineated the rules for law enforcement stops and searches of vehicles. The Court has permitted stops if officers have cause to believe that a crime has been committed, including any traffic violation. (11)

Once a car has been stopped, the driver and passengers can be ordered to stand outside the vehicle (for the officer's protection) without any objective showing of harm or danger. (12) At any time during the encounter—even after a ticket or warning has been issued—the police can secure consent to search the car or its occupants without advising the driver or passengers that consent need not be given or that they are free to leave. (13) Any contraband that is observed in "plain view," including anything pinpointed by flashlight, can be seized and used as probable cause to arrest. (14)

During the stop, anyone who appears dangerous may be frisked for the officer's protection. (15) If cause is established to arrest any of the occupants, a full-scale search of the car—including suitcases and other private containers—and of all other passengers is permissible. (16)

In Whren v. United States, officers made a traffic stop and observed two bags of crack cocaine in the hands of a front-seat passenger. (17) The police testified that they stopped the driver for violating several traffic laws. The defendants claimed that the stop was pretextual; that the police were suspicious because they observed two African-American men in a Nissan Pathfinder in Southeast Washington and that they alleged traffic violations so that they could conduct a drug investigation.

The Supreme Court ruled that from a Fourth Amendment perspective, the "constitutional reasonableness of traffic stops [does not depend] on the actual motivations of the individual officers." (18) The only relevant question was whether the officer had legal cause for the stop.

In response to the claim that pretextual stops could be racially motivated, the Court stated that the Equal Protection Clause of the Fourteenth Amendment would prohibit any intentional race discrimination in a car stop. Intentional race discrimination may be shown by a law that "expressly classifies persons on the basis of race." When there is no direct proof of such a policy or practice, statistical evidence must show that the police acted with the intent to discriminate. The Supreme Court has sustained attacks on racially discriminatory jury selection procedures and racially based peremptory challenges, using statistical evidence demonstrating that race played an impermissible role in these proceedings. (19)

However, in McCleskey v. Kemp, the Court rejected, as insufficient under Eighth and Fourteenth Amendment standards, a statistical analysis concerning the application of the death penalty in Georgia. (20) The study found that the race of the victim was consistently the most important factor in influencing a jury to impose the death penalty. If the victim was white, the odds of a defendant's receiving the death penalty were 4.3 times higher than if the victim was African-American.

The Court questioned how far the logic of the argument would carry: The claim, Justice Lewis Powell stated, "throws into serious question the principles that underlie our entire criminal justice system." (21) Justice William Brennan, dissenting, commented that the Court's concern with the implications of the statistics for other aspects of the criminal justice system displayed "a fear of too much justice." (22)

The Court took a similar hands-off approach in United States v. Armstrong, reversing a ruling that would have permitted discovery in support of a motion to dismiss federal crack cocaine prosecutions against African-American defendants on grounds of racially selective prosecution. (23) The Court stated that prosecutors were entitled to a presumption that they performed their duties properly. It relied on arrest statistics to reject the argument that blacks and whites commit drug offenses at rates that would not justify the highly disproportionate federal prosecution of African-American crack cocaine offenders.

McCleskey and Armstrong are troubling, but they are not dispositive of racial profiling claims. In McCleskey, the Court—in requiring proof beyond statistical patterns for the whole system to show that the judgment in an individual case was infected by intentional discrimination—stressed the unique discretion given juries to decide between life and death.

Armstrong's requirement that the defendant show that similarly situated white offenders were not subjected to federal prosecution, while questionable, should not bar selective policing claims. Evidence that shows a statistical disparity in the rates at which similarly situated black and white drivers are stopped and/or searched for alleged traffic violations establishes the factual basis for the claim. (24)

When a racial profiling challenge is based on the theory that official policy contains an express racial classification, there should be no need to prove the existence of a similar nonminority group or person who was not subjected to the practices. (25)

PEDESTRIAN STOPS

Pedestrian stops can be triggered by any number of factors, although legally, police officers cannot forcibly stop or detain people without reasonable suspicion of criminal conduct. The complexity of on-the-street investigations, from the perspectives of both race and crime control, makes legal and political judgments in this field controversial.

The seeds of constitutional controversy were planted in 1968 in Terry v. Ohio. (26) The Supreme Court ruled that a stop is reasonable under the Fourth Amendment if the facts and circumstances provide grounds for an officer to believe, objectively, that criminal activity is afoot. The Court decided that if the officer had a reasonable belief that the person stopped was armed and dangerous, he or she could conduct a pat-down frisk, again on less than probable cause.

Since Terry, the Court has significantly expanded police powers (often in deference to the war on drugs), and complaints concerning racial bias and arbitrary stops and frisks continue to mount.

While the issues of both complaints are often addressed as distinct constitutional matters, police investigative detentions often include both. For example, in Brown v. City of Oneonta, a police manhunt followed the assault of an elderly woman in that New York town. (27) She told the police that her attacker was "a young black man" who had cut his hand during the incident. Fewer than 300 African-Americans lived in town, and approximately 2 percent of the students at a nearby state university were black. The police made a sweep of the town, stopping and questioning more than 200 African-American men and inspecting their hands for cuts.

In a civil rights suit, the Second Circuit ruled that if police had a racial description and a relatively small number of possible suspects—even though there was no description beyond race and age—investigating all African-American men did not constitute intentional race discrimination.

Having isolated and rejected race as a constitutional problem, the court proceeded to analyze the Fourth Amendment claims to determine whether the police "seized" any of the plaintiffs. The court recognized that the description of "a young black man" was too vague to justify a stop. It also found that a police officer's pointing a spotlight at the plaintiff and saying, "What, are you stupid? Come here. I want to talk to you," and instructing him to show his hands constituted a seizure.

Brown's equal protection analysis finesses the difficult issues. The fact that a description of a suspect includes a racial characteristic should be merely the start of the analysis. Race is surely an appropriate consideration in such an investigation, but when it becomes the predominant factor, strict scrutiny applies.

A court should consider what other descriptive characteristics are known, the number of potential suspects, and the intrusiveness of the police investigation. Possibly, the court should distinguish between benign forms of investigation (for example, a written request that a person speak with the police) and a physical confrontation or forcible stop. The disquiet that Brown produces results from the artificial doctrinal lines that the Supreme Court has drawn around the Fourth and Fourteenth Amendments.

REMEDIES

Legislation and the courts have limited some of the traditional legal remedies in racial profiling cases.

Suppression of Evidence.   The exclusionary rule provides a remedy for some individual victims of illegal stops but does not provide systemic relief from racial profiling and random stop-and-frisk practices. Racially discriminatory stops are not subject to the Fourth Amendment exclusionary rule in selective prosecution cases, and the Supreme Court has yet to recognize a suppression remedy under the Fourteenth Amendment. Moreover, since most people subjected to these practices are not arrested, the matter never reaches criminal adjudication.

A notable exception is State v. Soto, the opening wedge in the New Jersey Turnpike racial profiling scandal. (28) Invoking liberal state discovery procedures in lawsuits alleging selective prosecution, the African-American defendants moved to suppress evidence that police obtained in a search of their vehicle. They presented evidence that African-Americans were being stopped at rates that far exceeded their use of the Turnpike. Police documents and statistical studies were sufficient to prove an extraordinary pattern of racial profiling, and the trial court suppressed the evidence in the cases.

Recently, a Pennsylvania appellate court sustained a suppression order in a criminal case in which it appeared that the police relied on the driver's race as a principal reason to stop a car. As the court stated, "driving while black" is not a violation of the motor vehicle code. (29)

The New Jersey Supreme Court has ruled that there can be no valid consent to a vehicle search after a traffic stop unless the police officer has reasonable grounds to believe that contraband or weapons are in the car. (30)

Civil Damages Actions. The Civil Rights Act—also known as [section] 1983—allows damages for harm caused by state or local officials' unconstitutional stops and searches. Claims against federal defendants (usually regarding border, customs, and airport searches) can be made under the Constitution as so-called Bivens actions or under the Federal Tort Claims Act. (31) Case law and commentary on [section] 1983 and Bivens actions are extensive. (32)

Briefly, damages actions can provide redress to those unlawfully stopped or searched, and they have the potential to trigger institutional reforms. When unconstitutional practices affect many people, as racial profiling and random stops and searches do, potential damages are substantial, and government agencies may seek to avoid large judgments by changing practices and policies. Proof of racial bias has led to significant damages in police misconduct cases. (33) In the highway racial profiling cases, significant settlements (often joined with affirmative relief by way of consent decree) have been effective in changing practices. (34)

Discovery rules broader than state or federal criminal discovery can be used to develop proof of patterns and practice in racial profiling. Section 1983 liability depends on proof that an individual officer violated a plaintiff's constitutional rights. In the racial profiling context, this requires evidence of intentional discrimination (often accompanied by Fourth Amendment violations regarding the stop and/or search). Qualified immunity may be introduced as a defense, but only where the officer reasonably believed that he or she was acting lawfully. Once intentional discrimination is proved, this defense is highly questionable. Claims against supervisors or municipalities are sustainable only if the constitutional violation was caused by a municipal law, policy, practice, or custom. (35)

Even if no contraband is found and there is a strong claim for damages, the amount may be too modest to justify full-scale litigation. The prospects change radically, however, if claims can be joined, and particularly if a class action can be built. Drug interdiction and related car and pedestrian stops may involve subjecting thousands of people to unlawful practices. The case for liability becomes exponentially stronger with the supportive allegations and testimony of hundreds or thousands of victims that the government has overreached, and the damages claims become substantial enough to sustain federal litigation.

Injunctive Relief.   Federal injunctive relief against state or local officers who violated federal constitutional or statutory rights is potentially the most effective remedy for preventing rights violations in the future. However, federal courts' powers are circumscribed by federalism, comity, and standing doctrines. (36)

In City of Los Angeles v. Lyons, the African-American plaintiff was stopped by city police officers for a traffic violation. (37) After Lyons got out of his car, the officers drew their guns, ordered him to place his hands on top of his head, and, without provocation, placed him in a chokehold, damaging his larynx. The Supreme Court ruled that Lyons had not proved a sufficient likelihood that he would again be subject to a police chokehold to request an injunction.

The Court distinguished Lyons in Friends of the Earth v. Laidlaw Environmental Services, granting federal standing under Article III to plaintiffs in an environmental lawsuit challenging the pollution of a river. (38) The plaintiffs alleged that they had suffered "injury in fact" because they were deterred from using the river for recreational purposes. The Court ruled that there was "nothing 'improbable' about the proposition that a company's continuous and pervasive discharge of pollutants into a river would cause nearby residents to curtail their recreational use of that waterway and would subject them to other economic and aesthetic harms." (39)

The Court ruled that Lyons did not bar the action because the unlawful conduct was occurring as the complaint was filed, a holding that confirms the significant difference between allegations of occasional unlawful conduct and practice-and-policy cases. Of course, a polluted river can affect everyone using it, while racial profiling on highways randomly affects thousands in a much larger class of drivers. The question becomes: Once a policy of racial profiling is established, is the probability that minorities will avoid certain highways or that certain members of the minority group will be stopped on those roads sufficient to establish standing?

In Lyons, the Court may have been reluctant to make a definitive ruling on chokeholds (which are permissible in some circumstances). But racial bias in policing cannot be justified, and permitting a challenge to such practices by someone who might not otherwise have standing to challenge police policies would be consistent with the Court's willingness to grant broad standing to challenge racially discriminatory practices. (40) Thus, while Lyons unjustifiably denies standing, it does not close the door to injunctive relief in the context of racial profiling.

FEDERAL INTERVENTION

The Violent Crime Control and Law Enforcement Act of 1994 authorizes the U.S. attorney general to bring civil actions for declaratory or equitable relief against police departments engaged in a pattern or practice of violating constitutional or statutory rights. (41) Since 1994, the Department of Justice has taken legal action against five law enforcement agencies. It has reached consent decrees with Pittsburgh, Pennsylvania; Steubenville, Ohio; and New Jersey (over racial profiling on the turnpike) and a settlement agreement with Montgomery County, Maryland (over racial profiling on I-95). It has also initiated litigation against the Columbus, Ohio, police department.

The New Jersey agreement prohibits troopers from considering the race, nationality, or ethnicity of turnpike motorists or passengers in determining which vehicles to stop or search, unless those factors were part of a suspect's description. The consent decree requires officers to record data on motor vehicle stops, including the gender and race or ethnicity of the driver and any passenger subjected to a "procedure," as well as the reason for the stop and any subsequent search. Supervisors must review troopers' reports on stops and may also review corresponding audio or video tapes. When a review reveals a possible violation of the decree, nondisciplinary action—such as counseling or more training—may be ordered. Similar provisions are incorporated in the Maryland agreement.

Three developments of the past few years have the potential to alter the legal and political landscape of contemporary policing practices.

First, there is almost universal condemnation of racial profiling. While debate over the exact definition of the term continues, there is growing support for the principle that race cannot be used to support a discretionary judgment by a police officer to stop, frisk, or search someone, except where a description of a suspect, including race, has been provided. Police departments will be pressed to adopt and implement policies prohibiting racial profiling, and courts are likely to intervene where patterns of racial profiling are proved.

Second, for the first time, reliable data are being collected and analyzed with respect to both racial disparities in stops and searches and whether adequate cause existed for the police intrusions. These data are essential to any serious effort to reconsider constitutional doctrine and address remedies for racial profiling and other arbitrary police conduct.

Third, police administrative measures that reflect a more progressive police management philosophy have been adopted. Ultimately, abuses will be significantly reduced only if these fundamental reforms in police policies and practices are fully implemented.

David Rudovsky is a senior fellow at the University of Pennsylvania Law School and a founding partner in Kairys, Rudovsky, Epstein & Messing of Philadelphia. Sections of this article were published in the February 2001 issue of the University of Pennsylvania Journal of Constitutional Law.

NOTES

1. Wilson v. Tinicum Township, No. Civ. A. 92-6617, 1993 WL 280205, at *2 (E.D. Pa. July 20, 1993) (opinion on class action certification).

2. State v. Soto, 734 A.2d 350, 360 (N.J. Super. Ct. Law Div. 1996).

3. PETER VERNIERO & PAUL H. ZOUBEK, INTERIM REPORT OF THE STATE POLICE REVIEW TEAM REGARDING ALLEGATIONS OF RACIAL PROFILING 26–28 (1999), available at www.state.nj.us/lps/intm_419.pdf [hereinafter NEW JERSEY INTERIM REPORT].

4. OFFICE OF THE ATTORNEY GENERAL OF NEW YORK STATE, REPORT ON THE NEW YORK CITY POLICE DEPARTMENT'S "STOP & FRISK" PRACTICES 88–89 (1999), available at www.oag.state.ny.us/press/reports/stop_frisk/stop_frisk.html.

5. A 1997 government survey found that the rate of illicit drug use for blacks was 7.5 percent; for whites, 6.4 percent; and for Hispanics, 5.9 percent. OFF. OF APPLIED STUD., U.S. DEP'T OF HEALTH & HUMAN SERVS., NATIONAL HOUSEHOLD SURVEY ON DRUG ABUSE (1997).

6. Ron Harris, Blacks Feel Brunt of Drug War, L.A. TIMES, Apr. 22, 1990, at A1.

7. NEW JERSEY INTERIM REPORT, supra note 3, at 67–68.

8. Id. at 26–28.

9. Report of John Lamberth, Md. State Conf. of NAACP Branches v. Md. Dep't of State Police, 72 F. Supp. 2d 560 (D. Md. 1999), available at www.aclu.org/court/lamberth.html.

10. Ira Glasser, ACLU Biennial Speech (June, 1999), available at www.aclu.org/issues/racial/bispeech99.html.

11. Whren v. United States, 517 U.S. 806, 816–19 (1996).

12. Maryland v. Wilson, 519 U.S. 408, 410 (1997).

13. Ohio v. Robinette, 519 U.S. 33 (1996).

14. Horton v. California, 496 U.S. 128, 133–37 (1990).

15. Michigan v. Long, 463 U.S. 1032, 1035 (1983).

16. Wyoming v. Houghton, 526 U.S. 295, 302–07 (1999).

17. 517 U.S. 806.

18. Id. at 813.

19. Batson v. Kentucky, 476 U.S. 79, 94–98 (1986).

20. 481 U.S. 279 (1987).

21. Id. at 314.

22. Id. at 339 (Brennan, J., dissenting).

23. 517 U.S. 456 (1996).

24. See Hunter v. Underwood, 471 U.S. 222 (1985) (relying on statistics in finding that a facially neutral disenfranchisement statute was in violation of the Equal Protection Clause of the Fourteenth Amendment).

25. Brown v. City of Oneonta, 221 F.3d 329, 337 (2d Cir. 2000); see, e.g., Rodriguez v. California Highway Patrol, 89 F. Supp. 2d 1131 (N.D. Cal. 2000) (allowing equal protection claim based in part on statistical evidence); Md. State Conf. of NAACP Branches, 72 F. Supp. 2d 560 (noting that plaintiffs have standing based on continuing practice of racial profiling by police); Nat'l Cong. for Puerto Rican Rights v. City of New York, 191 F.R.D. 52 (S.D.N.Y. 1999) (holding that allegation that police stopped and frisked African-American

and Latino men based on their race and national origin was sufficient to state equal protection claim).

26. 392 U.S. 1 (1968).

27. 221 F.3d 329.

28. 734 A.2d 350.

29. Commonwealth v. Palmer, 751 A.2d 223 (Pa. Super. Ct. 2000).

30. State v. Carty, 790 A.2d 903 (N.J. Mar. 4, 2002).

31. Bivens v. Six Unknown Fed. Narcotics Agents, 403 U.S. 388 (1971) (recognizing Fourth Amendment cause of action brought directly under the U.S. Constitution).

32. See MICHAEL AVERY ET AL., POLICE MISCONDUCT: LAW AND LITIGATION (3d ed., 2002).

33. E.g., Price v. Kramer, 200 F.3d 1237 (9th Cir. 1999); Morgan v. Woessner, 997 F.2d 1244 (9th Cir. 1993); Hall v. Ochs, 817 F.2d 920 (1st Cir. 1987).

34. See, e.g., Robert Jackson, Eagle County Must Pay for Stopping Motorists, ROCKY MOUNTAIN NEWS, Nov. 10,1995, at A4 (reporting settlement of racial profiling claim based on litigation, Whitfield v. Board of County Comm'rs, 837 F. Supp. 338 (D. Colo. 1993)); Settlement Agreement, Wilson v. Tinicum Township, No. 92-6617 (E.D. Pa. Jan. 19, 1995).

35. Board of County Comm'rs v. Brown, 520 U.S. 397 (1997); City of Canton v. Harris, 489 U.S. 378 (1959); Monell v. Dep't of Soc. Servs., 436 U.S. 658 (1928).

36. Lewis v. Casey, 518 U.S 343 (1996); City of Los Angeles v. Lyons, 461 U.S. 95 (1983).

37. 461 U.S. 95.

38. 528 U.S. 167 (2000).

39. Id. at 184.

40. See Shaw v. Hunt, 517 U.S. 899, 904–05 (1996); Powers v. Ohio, 499 U.S. 400 (1991).

41. 42 U.S.C. [section] 14141 (1995).

InfoMarks: Make Your Mark

What Is an InfoMark?

It is a single-click return ticket to any page, any result, or any search from InfoTrac College Edition.

An InfoMark is a stable URL, linked to InfoTrac College Edition articles that you have selected. InfoMarks can be used like any other URL, but they're better because they're stable—they don't change. Using an InfoMark is like performing the search again whenever you follow the link, whether the result is a single article or a list of articles.

How Do InfoMarks Work?

If you can "copy and paste," you can use InfoMarks.

When you see the InfoMark icon on a result page, its URL can be copied and pasted into your electronic document—web page, word processing document, or email. Once InfoMarks are incorporated into a document, the results are persistent (the URLs will not change) and are dynamic.

Even though the saved search is used at different times by different users, an InfoMark always functions like a brand new search. Each time a saved search is executed, it accesses the latest updated information. That means subsequent InfoMark searches might yield additional or more up-to-date information than the original search with less time and effort.

Capabilities

InfoMarks are the perfect technology tool for creating:

- Virtual online readers
- Current awareness topic sites—links to periodical or newspaper sources
- Online/distance learning courses
- Bibliographies, reference lists
- Electronic journals and periodical directories
- Student assignments
- Hot topics

Advantages

- Select from over 15 million articles from more than 5,000 journals and periodicals
- Update article and search lists easily
- Articles are always full-text and include bibliographic information
- All articles can be viewed online, printed, or emailed
- Saves professors and students time
- Anyone with access to InfoTrac College Edition can use it
- No other online library database offers this functionality
- FREE!

How to Use InfoMarks

There are three ways to utilize InfoMarks—in HTML documents, Word documents, and Email

HTML Document

1. Open a new document in your HTML editor (Netscape Composer or FrontPage Express).
2. Open a new browser window and conduct your search in InfoTrac College Edition.
3. Highlight the URL of the results page or article that you would like to InfoMark.
4. Right-click the URL and click Copy. Now, switch back to your HTML document.
5. In your document, type in text that describes the InfoMarked item.
6. Highlight the text and click on Insert, then on Link in the upper bar menu.
7. Click in the link box, then press the "Ctrl" and "V" keys simultaneously and click OK. This will paste the URL in the box.
8. Save your document.

Word Document

1. Open a new Word document.
2. Open a new browser window and conduct your search in InfoTrac College Edition.
3. Check items you want to add to your Marked List.
4. Click on Mark List on the right menu bar.
5. Highlight the URL, right-click on it, and click Copy. Now, switch back to your Word document.
6. In your document, type in text that describes the InfoMarked item.
7. Highlight the text. Go to the upper bar menu and click on Insert, then on Hyperlink.

8. Click in the hyperlink box, then press the "Ctrl" and "V" keys simultaneously and click OK. This will paste the URL in the box.
9. Save your document.

Email

1. Open a new email window.
2. Open a new browser window and conduct your search in InfoTrac College Edition.
3. Highlight the URL of the results page or article that you would like to InfoMark.
4. Right-click the URL and click Copy. Now, switch back to your email window.
5. In the email window, press the "Ctrl" and "V" keys simultaneously. This will paste the URL into your email.
6. Send the email to the recipient. By clicking on the URL, he or she will be able to view the InfoMark.